Make Money, Think Rich

How to Use Behavioral Finance Principles to Become Rich

Dale Buckner, CFP®

First Edition Design Publishing
Sarasota, Florida USA

Make Money, Think Rich
How to Become Rich Using Behavioral Finance Principles

Copyright ©2014, 2022 Dale Buckner

ISBN 978-1506-910-92-5 HC
ISBN 978-1506-910-93-2 PBK
ISBN 978-1506-910-94-9 EBK

LCCN 2014948450

October, 2014, 2022

Published and Distributed by
First Edition Design Publishing, Inc.
P.O. Box 20217, Sarasota, FL 34276-3217
www.firsteditiondesignpublishing.com

I dedicate this book to our family, the Buckner clan, which can be traced back to 1570 England. I wonder if a member of our family saw an original Shakespeare play?

The dedication continues through today, to our four grandchildren, Arzana, Roland, Adria, and Rhys...and to every teacher, artist, poet, lawyer, banker, and advisor in between.

Acknowledgements

First, my wife Adair and family, for allowing me the freedom to pursue my dream. Your support has meant the world to me.

Our son, Dr. Cameron Buckner, who helped transform the book into a much more scholarly endeavor. His PhD in Cognitive Science and keen insights into how the brain makes decisions has transformed virtually every page of the book. The book couldn't make it into print without his help.

Danielle Buckner Skala, M.Ed., BCBA, LBA who directs a clinic for autistic children. She helped me understand how to change inappropriate behavior.

Fritz Meyer, for his help and encouragement. It's always helpful to have a nationally renowned economist on your side. Mr. Meyer contributed generously in providing current economic data.

Dr. Matt Medeiros, for his early encouraging words, helping to bring my ideas to the page. His insights into managing money helped to mold more than one chapter.

A heartfelt thank you goes to my editor, Michael Dubes. His gentle counsel and encouragement was and is much appreciated.

I wish to thank my clients, radio show listeners, fellow financial planners, and everyone who listened to my theories until the story was finally told on these pages.

Foreword

Over the past 40 years, the stock market has delivered approximately 10% compounded annually. Someone investing just $1,000 a year and retiring at the end of that period would have accumulated $443,000. Investing $2,000 a year certainly a manageable amount for most baby boomers. Any retirement saver would have an accumulation of $886,000.

The almost magical power of long-term compounding allows anyone to achieve the goal of saving enough for retirement. Yet we read about legions of frightened baby boomers, afraid they will outlive the meager savings they've managed to set aside.

The question is why? Why have so many Americans come up short when they easily could have saved enough for a comfortable retirement?

The answer is what I call "investor bad behavior." So many people make crucial behavioral mistakes during their accumulation years. And in most cases, they have no one to blame but themselves.

As an economist and stock market strategist, I've met thousands of financial advisors during my career and I've concluded that some advisors offer significantly more value than others. They are the advisors who effectively execute two distinct assignments for their clients: one technical and one psychological.

The technical piece is the discipline of Modern Portfolio Theory. Advisors delivering value avoid trying to beat the market with the tactical asset allocation guesswork that is so prevalent among the "experts" on Wall Street and the financial news networks. Many advisors, being human after all, want to appear smart, so they make these types of bets with their clients' money in order to impress. Big mistake. I've observed that it's often the old dogs in the business that have learned this lesson the hard way. Some of the young dogs...not so much.

Getting the technical piece right takes smarts, hard work, dedication, and experience. Unfortunately, some advisors think that if they do this piece well their job is done. But it's the second piece — the crucial psychological piece — that is often overlooked or eludes the advisor.

The psychological piece is instilling the conviction that staying the course with an investment program based on Modern Portfolio Theory is critical to long-term success.

Sounds simple, staying the course. But it isn't. Not by a long shot. Remember the crash of 2008-09. In this book, Dale Buckner recalls helping a panic-stricken client at the bear-market bottom. "That was the day he almost became poor forever." Here was a man who just couldn't bear to watch the value of his nest egg contract any further. On his own, I have little doubt he would have capitulated at or near the bottom and he would, indeed, have become poor forever. That story had a happy ending because, like a great athlete, the advisor came up with a key play in the clutch. He earned many times his keep by keeping his client invested through that epic market collapse.

I can't overstate the importance of an advisor's ability to educate and counsel clients on the stay-the-course imperative. You can get all the technical aspects of investing right but if in the clutches of a bear market you get the psychological piece wrong, you're toast.

Dale Buckner understands this and has blessed us with this insightful and entertaining treatise on how we're seemingly "hard-wired" to do the dumb things that prevent us from investing successfully. Using comprehensive research, he shows us how to allow the deceptively simple practice of consistent saving and compounding to get the job done. I hope you'll enjoy his observations as much as I have.

Fritz Meyer
Economist and former Senior Marketing Strategist for Invesco

Make Money, Think Rich

How to Use Behavioral Finance Principles to
Become Rich

Dale Buckner, CFP®

Contents

Prologue

Pandemics, Politics, and Human Nature

This book employs scientific evidence to examine why humans tend to make poor investment choices. Most investors continue to see their investment results harmed by the book's two main themes: fear and greed. Fear and greed are human emotions that are as old as history, even prehistory. The Bible also cites fear, greed, envy and desire as destructive influences so this has been going on for a long time.

These emotions are so deeply rooted and strong. Unless recognized and dealt with appropriately emotions will keep you from reaching your investment goals. Humans are hardwired to sell at the bottom and buy at the peak of a market cycle.

Don't think that the news will help you determine the direction of the next market cycle. Fear or greed often will convince an investor to sell out at the bottom of a market correction. Many investors buy at the top of a speculative bubble. The news feeds the destructive impulses. Take a moment to reflect that the media isn't your friend. Stop, reflect and take a deep breath. In the book I call that step "pause and reflect."

We humans are flawed. Our imperfections show up in the way we invest. With training, an investor can build good investment habits. Trust in the process as you read about our ancestor's trials and triumphs. Perhaps you will see how the pieces all fit together.

In conclusion, humans are not created with flaws. We are not mistakes. We are this way for a reason. We were given free will and the ability to learn and profit from the mistakes of others. Once you've gotten good at it, it is your duty to spread the good word to your fellow Homo Sapiens and show them the way.

Ancestral Life

The National Geographic Genographic Project explored the DNA of people around the world. Approximately 60,000 years ago, anatomically modern man began migrating from the African continent. Our migrating ancestors were gifted with intelligence similar to what we have today. These men and women migrating out of Africa were clever survivors. They were us just a scant 1,500 lifetimes ago—a blink of an eye in evolutionary time.

The minds we possess today are comprised of a mosaic of behaviors and biases developed during our evolution. Our ancestors had to solve a variety of problems and survive diverse and challenging environments. The archeological evidence in this area is incomplete. What do we know about some of our more recent relatives?

Scientists estimate that the genus Homo, which includes our more recent human ancestors, diverged from a common ancestor shared with chimpanzees around 5-7 million years ago. They then went through a series of intense evolutionary changes. The oldest hominid skeleton yet found—a female member of the species Ardipithecus ramidus nicknamed "Ardi". Ardi had already gone through some of the evolutionary changes that characterize modern humans.

Discovered in Ethiopia in 1994, Ardi's age has been estimated at 4.4 million years. Her body is similar to those of other modern apes like chimpanzees and baboons. Fully grown, she weighed a mere 110 pounds, was about four feet tall and had a brain roughly 1/5 the size of modern humans. However, the bones in Ardi's pelvis and limbs had already shifted to allow her to walk upright. She also possessed other characteristics, such as decreased canine tooth size and body development. Scientists suggest Ardi's troop lived a more human-like social structure.

Ardi's world was becoming less like one ruled by one big male who beat up the other males and got to breed with all the women (a societal structure modern humans now restrict to a period during adolescence called "high school"). Ardi's troop was moving toward a society based around mate pair-bonding. Parental investment in raising young could now become a primary family focus.

Ardi's closest ancestors were mostly vegetarian, tree-dwelling foragers living at the intersections of forests in Africa. Scientists theorize that around that time a series of drastic climatic changes forced our ancestors out of the tree canopy and down to the ground. As they moved out of the trees and onto the savanna, they exposed themselves to new dangers.

Several skulls have been found with teeth marks indicating Ardi's troop faced predation. Dinofelis, a form of saber-toothed cat too large (estimated at 275 pounds) to climb trees could kill members of the troop quickly with a brutal chomp to the head or neck.

These pressures began to favor increased intelligence to avoid predators. Locating food in changing environments became difficult. Our ancestors needed to collaborate in social groups to survive. As their skulls expanded to meet this demand for greater smarts, our ancestors apparently began to scavenge meat. Our relatives began using stone tools to carve animal carcasses, a change some anthropologists ascribe to the need to feed the higher caloric demands of a bigger brain.

The challenges facing our ancestors were severe, including predators, rapid climatic shifts, starvation, and battles with other hominids. Some of the climatic changes are hard to imagine in modern terms.

One hypothesis, called the Toba Catastrophe, holds that a super volcanic eruption in Indonesia 77,000 years ago belched enough dust into the atmosphere to cause a 6–10-year volcanic winter. With so much dust in the atmosphere, sunlight would have been blocked and global temperatures would have plummeted. This can be partially verified through geological evidence and ice core samples.

In turn, these changes would have killed off a great percentage of the world's plants and animals. Genetic evidence suggests that our ancestors may have been reduced to as few as 10,000 breeding individuals, producing a "genetic bottleneck." Such bottlenecks increase the chances of species change and adaptation. Individuals possessing beneficial traits can be among the only ones to survive.

Useful genes and skills can quickly spread through a small population through reproduction. Sometime shortly afterward, humanity began to pour out of Africa to populate the world. Humans brought tools, fire, clothing, language, and all the other trappings of modern Homo sapiens.

The science that attempts to understand how our modern mental capacities were shaped by the challenges faced by our ancestors is called evolutionary psychology. The driving forces behind evolution are differential survival and reproduction.

Animals with traits and strategies that allow them to succeed in their environments will tend to survive and reproduce. Animals who lack them will tend to die out. When faced with survival pressures over time, more beneficial traits can spread throughout the population.

The basic idea of evolutionary psychology holds that many of our modern psychological traits can be explained as adaptations to the historical conditions in which we evolved. In other words, if we want to understand why we do something today, we can ask whether our ancestors might have used that strategy to address a challenge in the environments in which they lived.

Trying to apply these evolved tools to problems that differ in their structure from the ancient ones for which they were designed can be like trying to put in screws with a hammer; not recommended.

For example, evolutionary psychologists have hypothesized that human beauty preferences might be an adaptation. Some psychologists have studied men's preference for women with the classic "hourglass" figure, described in terms of a measurement called the waist-to-hip ratio (WHR). When surveyed, men tend to favor a low WHR of about .7, meaning they like women with comparatively larger hips and smaller waistlines.[1] Notably, many beauty icons have a WHR of .7 or lower despite having very different heights and body fat percentages. These include Marilyn Monroe, Sophia Loren, Chrissy Teigen, Kim Kardashian or Jessica Alba.

There are several possible evolutionary explanations for these preferences. For one, WHR tends to be a very good marker for estrogen blood levels, providing visual signs of fertility.

For another, as our brains expanded during evolution, so did our babies' skulls. An increased birth canal size became very important for hominid childbirth, and so "child-bearing hips" would have been a big plus. Also, women with lower WHR tend to live longer, healthier lives, and researchers have even argued that the fatty acids stored in those hips might provide the raw material for healthier fetal brain development, leading to smarter offspring.

All this suggests that men with a WHR preference of .7 or lower would tend to choose reproductively better mates, and so reproduce more successfully, than those who liked flatter or more rounded figures.

Evolutionary psychology is not without its detractors. One objection is that, too often, evolutionary stories about modern capacities are accepted because they paint a vivid picture of life on the ancient African savanna, rather than being based on hard archaeological or biological evidence. Evolutionary psychology also seems to display an "obsession with the Pleistocene." This is the period from about 2.5 million years ago to the present during which hominids began to emerge from our most recent ancestors.

Our time as hominids was clearly important in forming our modern human bodies and mental capacities. Even Ardi was already endowed with a host of psychological capacities inherited from her more distant ancestors. Some of those capacities, such as basic emotions, have been retained in mammals in a relatively unchanged form for nearly 70 million years. In other words, studying the environments faced by ancient mice can sometimes be as relevant to understanding modern human psychology as studying those faced by ancient apes.

Finally, sometimes our behavioral traits are just unavoidable by-products or arise from random chance. For example, rather than assuming that flatulence served as some kind of ideal predator-repelling device during the Pleistocene, we might just accept it as the unfortunate byproduct of the chemistry of digestion.

Every human today is operating with a body and mind that evolved to suit a profoundly different environment than the one in which we live in today. We use the same brain and body today to decide whether to buy stocks, bonds or real estate. Our ancestors had to decide whether to fight a predator or run. On a good day they decided to keep foraging for food at the current site or to pick up and move to another site or what kind of tool to bring on the big hunt.

Applying this knowledge can help you understand your own destructive investment behaviors and biases. These behaviors might have been survival skills during different situations of the past. The hopeful result is that you can better control those behaviors in our new, modern circumstances.

Introduction

Some people get rich studying artificial intelligence.
Me, I make my money studying natural stupidity.

Carl Icahn

On March 9, 2009, the S&P 500 Index touched 666.79, the lowest point of the so-called "Great Recession." Tracking that index, a portfolio at its October 2007 high of $100,000 would have been worth just $42,600 if sold at the market bottom in March 2009, a loss of 58.4 percent.

Had it not been sold, that portfolio would have rebounded to be worth $132,000 on March 1, 2014, if the owner had reinvested the approximately 2.5 percent dividends. If instead that money had been taken out of the stock market at the bottom and placed in personal savings or bonds—perceived as "safe harbors" at the time—most of the 58.4 percent loss would have been locked in, the money gone forever.

This investment behavior—selling out at or near a market bottom and moving to low-yield investments thought to be safe—is an irrational response to a market downturn. You couldn't devise a worse trading strategy if you tried. Yet millions of investors did just that: took their money out at the absolute market bottom.

They stuffed it under the proverbial mattress and locked in their losses. Even more amazingly, many of these trades were executed under the advice of stockbrokers and financial planners. These trained advisors should have known better.

Of course, the investors and advisors who sold stocks on March 9, 2009 didn't know that day would mark the bottom of the recession stock selloff. They didn't have a crystal ball. Nobody does. And if someone claims to be able to predict market bottoms for you, run from their office as fast as you can.

The millions of investors who sold at the bottom thought stocks were going to keep going down. Given the hysteria of the time, they probably thought the financial collapse of the entire world was right around the corner.

Nearly 7.7 billion NYSE and NASDAQ listed shares were sold on March 9, 2009. Similar behavior happens every recession. By definition, a market bottom is created by billions of such ill-fated trades. Repeatedly, investors and advisers alike do the exact opposite of what history and common sense tell them they should do. How are such irrational decisions even possible?

Many books have been written about market cycles. Market cycles are normal and have occurred many times in the past. Most investors who sold on March 9 had lived through at least one such cycle and seen the market recover from recession, however dire.

In retrospect, they no doubt recognized that the market regularly goes through and recovers from downturns. They might even admit that the smarter strategy would be to invest more money at the bottom. Taking money out of the stock market after a steep downturn isn't on my successful investor's strategy list.

On the day they liquidated their stock, with panic in their hearts and a queasy feeling in the pits of their stomachs, they reasoned that this time, it was different.

Some people seem unable to learn from the past. When it comes to investing, irrational behavior is the norm. Like a computer with a virus, are investors programmed to crash? Are you doomed to repeat their mistakes, or can you benefit from their destructive behaviors and biases?

The problem isn't a shortage of good advice. Bookstores are crammed with volumes on investment and personal finance. In terms of strategy, they all offer similar guidance: eliminate debt, maintain a balanced and diversified portfolio, and don't buy into bubbles or sell during panics. If investors simply followed these simple rules, there would be a lot less volatility in the market and a lot more wealth in investors' pockets. So, shouldn't the problem have already been solved by now?

Good investment strategy is only part of the solution. The heart of the problem isn't that people don't know how to invest but rather that they don't know why they don't invest as they know they should.

To break free of that destructive behavior, we must first understand its causes. Only by understanding the nature of these destructive impulses can we take control of our investment behavior. We can stop making the same mistakes over and over again.

Moreover—and this is the fun part—if we understand the reasons why other investors fail, we can take advantage of their repetitive irrational behavior. We can benefit from the poor decision-making of our fellow investors who can't resist the natural tendency to buy high and sell low.

To a large extent, investors fail because of deep-rooted impulses and instincts inherited from genetic ancestors. Primitive survival instincts hardwired into investors' behavior compel them to do exactly the opposite of what would make them money.

Most are instinctually compelled to behavioral patterns that cause them to commit the same investment errors. Primal fears force investors out of the stock market at a time when they should be moving into stocks. When they should be selling, their decision-making process is frozen because they are certain their investments will go higher still.

Behavioral Finance and Psychological Finance sciences have begun to unravel through experiments what behaviors investors repeatedly exhibit that interfere with good investment results. Why we do what we do can best be explained with Evolutionary science.

These investment instincts of the human animal have been forged by millions of years of evolution. We shouldn't be embarrassed; these are the same instincts that helped our ancestors survive through brutally difficult conditions.

Consider this amazing fact: that you are here today represents the success of every single one of your ancestors. They all had to be healthy and successful enough to survive predators, secure food, impress a mate, reproduce and protect their young to adulthood.

If each hadn't managed to perform all these feats, through thousands of generations, you wouldn't be here today. We should all take a moment to congratulate ourselves on having such skillful and intrepid kin.

Unfortunately, the same instincts that ensured the survival of our ancestors now jeopardize 21st century investment decisions. It should be no surprise that these impulses are inappropriate in our modern investment environment.

Humans spent millions of years adapting to life as hunters and gatherers in the forests and savannahs of Africa. The modern stock market has existed for less than 150 years—a blink of the eye in evolutionary time.

401k investments have been around since 1978, and computer programmed trading, which can generate unfathomable amounts of data throughout the 24-hour day business cycle, has existed for less than three decades.

Though we're capable of learning to override and control our instincts—which I'll help you do in this book—most families have little or no prior experience in making crucial investment decisions.

Even those with decades of experience, like the stockbrokers who told their clients to sell on March 9, 2009, have the deck stacked against them. Our brains are full of ancient programming or biases that inhibit us from learning from our mistakes.

A personal aside: I started writing this book at the height of the stock market crash of 2008-2009. One of my clients, we will call him Ralph, had lost roughly 50 percent of his account's value by December of 2008. Despite this, his portfolio contained quality investments that continued to pay a consistent income, his reason for choosing the investments in the first place. In fact, his account enjoyed a rising income while dropping in value due to professional management.

Ralph was literally shaking when he arrived at my office. He said he hadn't been able to sleep, worrying about the drop in his account's value. "What if it goes down another 50 percent?" he gasped. "My account would be worthless. I have to sell out; I feel like I will die if I don't.'"

I told him, "I understand. These are very real feelings, but you own good stuff and your income is even better today. Just as important, your account will likely be worth more a year from now. The key is that your income stream is secure. Don't listen to the crazy people on TV and don't look at your statement for a while."

Ralph let me keep his account intact. It rebounded in value and a year later was worth more than when he bought it. Ralph became a believer. We laugh about it now but that was the day that he almost became poor forever.

In short, we simply can't hope to have adapted to modern investment conditions in such a short period of evolutionary time. Despite knowing what we ought to do when the news gets too bad or too good, we revert to our earlier biases and behavior scripts.

In our natural environments we might have earned the name given to us by biologists—Homo sapiens, meaning "wise man".

When it comes to investment decisions, a different name seems more appropriate. Let's call the investors who let their instincts cause them to buy high and sell low Homo pauperis, or "paupers" for short.

Homo pauperis were discovered only in the last few decades. Paupers are hominids with an average height of about 5'9" and lifespan of around 84 years. They are social animals, living in large communities with other members of their species.

Paupers have highly developed brains and can be distinguished by their skill with tools and language. They build fires, cook their food, make and wear clothing and have a variety of sophisticated technologies to control their natural environment.

As mammals, they wean their young, who have an extended (and expensive) adolescence lasting up until the age of twenty. There are recent reports of some adolescences lasting much longer.

Unlike most species, which have a natural environment to which they are well adapted, paupers are mostly found in artificial environments, shelters they call supermarkets, malls and stock exchanges. Paupers exhibit some of their most distinctive characteristics in a dwelling called a casino but more about that later.

In these respects, paupers are much like their nearest relatives, Homo sapiens. There is one key difference, however, which can best be observed when the two species receive a quarterly investment statement reporting a large loss. Homo sapiens react to a market downturn calmly because their investment decisions are based on sound strategy and calculation.

Paupers react the same way they would respond to a charging rhinoceros: racing pulse, sweaty palms, and panic. Blood rushes to their arms and legs. They are prepared to fight the quarterly statement to the death.

Flooded with adrenaline and other stress hormones, they are susceptible to making impulsive investment decisions with destructive consequences.

Making all this worse, Homo sapiens in the media often prey upon this weakness in the paupers by using ominous headlines and dire predictions to frighten them into selling their investments at the worst time. (Greedy Homo sapiens who work in finance can greatly profit from this practice by selling short or banking hefty commissions on the sale of the terrified paupers' stocks.) Over the long term, paupers tend to squander their hard-earned wealth in this manner and end up...well, as poor as paupers.

Fortunately, we hominids don't have to invest like paupers, or undergo the lengthy process of genetic evolution to find better strategies. We just need to pay attention to our mistakes and get smarter.

An APT Strategy

This book will explain how to take advantage of the predictable failures of most investors. You will learn why most investors, advisors and even institutional investment managers act less like wise investors and more like a bunch of monkeys in suits.

My goal is to help you understand and take control of the ancient instincts that doom so many to financial failure. Throughout the book, you will find simple rules that can help you break out of your destructive investment patterns.

You can outperform those who are programmed to approach investing like they are hunting and foraging rather than investing their assets for long-term maturity in the modern world.

I call this strategy APT decision-making: Acknowledge, Pause and Think.

The first step in breaking out of an instinctive behavioral pattern is to Acknowledge that you are in it. This is harder than you might think. One reason why our evolved behavioral patterns were so effective in past environments is that they are largely automatic and happen quickly.

When faced with true danger, we react before we are even aware of our actions. We respond to threats with the required speed, without engaging in slow, deliberate reflection.

It would be difficult to hit prey with a spear or dodge an enemy's blow if we consciously thought about the pros and cons of every possible action before moving our bodies.

Our ancestors would have starved or had their brains knocked out thousands of years ago if they reacted slowly. For this reason, our instincts and biases often take control of our behavior before cooler heads have a chance to prevail.

With practice, we can break out of these automated behavior patterns and override them. The first step is to understand these instinctual responses and biases so we can Acknowledge their signs. Even the most seasoned financial advisors can fall prey to destructive behavioral patterns. They don't realize they are in their grip.

To an investor experiencing a panicked flight response, selling at any price appears to be the logical response to the current threat. But once we acknowledge that we are under the influence of an evolved response or bias, we can start to break out of it.

Understanding our natural impulses and biases is important. The first half of this book is structured around the evolved patterns and behaviors that you must learn to recognize in order to become a successful investor.

The second step in our cycle is to Pause. Our evolved responses are not easily overcome. Many are what biologists refer to as ballistic, like a gunshot: once fired, they tend toward completion without any conscious monitoring or maintenance.

Again, this is something that was once useful. An ancestor who didn't stop running from a predator until well out of danger was less likely to be eaten than his buddy who suddenly halted halfway to safety to wonder if he should keep running. He ruined his chances of becoming anybody's ancestor.

Moreover, these responses are not just psychological but physiological. During a fight or flight response, our bodies go through a long list of changes that can affect our decision-making for hours afterward.

Even after you've acknowledged that you're in a panic, you won't be able to think clearly until you've lowered your heart rate and allowed your levels of adrenaline and other stress hormones to return to baseline.

The trick to the Pause step is to train ourselves to go to an appropriate frame of mind that will help us break out of the destructive behavioral pattern that we've Acknowledged.

When in a panic caused by a market crash, this might mean turning off your television, laptop, and cell phone and imagining yourself in a place of peace and tranquility. For me, it's a beautiful sunny day in the South Pacific, swaying in a hammock to a light breeze, sipping fresh coconut juice—but to each their own.

When tempted to buy into a bubble, this might mean stepping away from the upward-spiking market graphs on TV and tempering your excitement by soberly remembering how terrible you felt during previous downturns.

This step often is called the balanced mind step. When you have equal parts of the greed and fear hormones, your mind and reasoning are balanced. The panicked investor might contemplate whether to invest now at the bottom of a stock market selloff. The investor at the top of a market bubble might contemplate loses.

The final step in your cycle is Think. It's the stage where you try to figure out if your evolved responses were appropriate, as well as what you should do next.

This step is easier than the others. The goal is not to predict the market, which is pretty much impossible anyway. But we don't have to: you can do quite well by overcoming your destructive tendencies and biases. Simply let your money sit still through downturns.

If left alone for 30 or 40 years, portfolios invested in broad stock indices tend to vastly outperform more active strategies. Of course, it's useful to have some mechanisms to determine whether we are in a bubble or a bust.

While no one can accurately predict the day-to-day action of the market, it's possible to recognize whether the paupers around us are caught in the grip of an irrational response pattern. This alone might be enough to tell you how you should act. I've included a series of guidelines throughout the book to help you diagnose when the paupers are going berserk.

With the basic framework in place, it's time to get to work. Let's see how Homo pauperis hunts and forages in an unnatural environment, the modern stock exchange. We'll discuss some of the basic behavioral patterns and biases derived from our ancestors' psychology, their origins, and how they can ruin our investments. Finally, I will help you learn how to APT-ly deal with them and avoid committing the same mistakes in the future.

Chapter One

Hunting and Gathering

The covetous man is ever in want.
Horace (65 BC-8 BC)

Before history could be recorded, our ancestors hoarded, coveted, collected, hunted and foraged. Food and game were often scarce. Tools had to be painstakingly made by hand out of materials that were sometimes hard to find.

They were always on the lookout for new sources of food and raw materials. When times were tough, even a few more calories or one extra arrow could mean the difference between death and survival. And times were often tough. If our ancestors weren't prepared, they could starve, be unable to defend themselves against attack, or even be unable to reproduce.

It's hard to know exactly what our ancestors' lives were like, but we can get some idea from contemporary hunter-gatherer societies like the Hazda people. They live around the Great Rift Valley of Tanzania.

The Hazda are last full-time hunter-gatherers in Africa and very nearly the last in the world. From the fossil record, we know that they now live in one of the very same areas where our early ancestors dwelled.

Genus Homo emerged around 2 million years. Organized agriculture developed only about 10,000 years ago. We hominids have spent over 99% of our evolutionary time living as hunter-gatherers. Most of this time was probably spent in conditions very much like those in which most Hazda still live today.

Scientists theorize that the Hazda have lived a stable nomadic lifestyle in a range around their current area for tens of thousands of years. They keep no livestock; they plant no crops; they build no permanent shelters. Both men and women forage.

Men tend to search alone for fruit and wild game. Women forage in groups for fruits and berries and dig for root vegetables. They move seasonally around the parched and semi-arid deserts of the Great Rift Valley and over the plateaus of the neighboring Serengeti. They adapt their hunting and foraging to wet and dry weather as conditions demand.

They make stone tools and have learned to coat their arrows with poison extracted from the desert rose to kill their prey more quickly. Men also occasionally hunt in groups for larger game, including their favorite treat, baboons. Their lives require little organized planning beyond the next hunt.

The Hazda train for years to survive in their harsh environment, which requires a kind of natural expertise few humans in the developed world could hope to match. They are expert foragers, able to interpret the song of the honeyguide bird to find rich caches of honey.

They are skilled archers and stealth hunters, lying for hours by water holes to snag large game, such as giraffes. They have been observed sneaking up at night on a tree full of sleeping baboons.

When the Hazda bring down a larger animal, they drag it back to camp and share in a communal feast. Skillful hunters are highly compensated. They receive rewards such as smoking pipes, tobacco, tribal status and the most alluring marriage opportunities.

Imagine what it would have been like for our ancestors who, starving for calories, got the first taste of a rich load of honeycomb. Imagine the exhilaration upon bringing down a big giraffe with enough protein to feed their tribe for weeks.

They would imprint the exact location, hunting strategy, weather conditions, and other details of the hunt's resulting wealth of resources. They would celebrate joyously and be applauded. In response to the rewards and accolades, they would try repeatedly to duplicate that success. They would risk mortal injury or death to feel that elation once again.

It is worth looking "under the hood" for a moment to see that many of these sensations are out of our control. The satisfaction of a set of basic needs—such as food, drink, and sex—are what psychologists call primary reinforcers.

Reinforcement is one of the foundational principles of psychology. The basic idea is that when a behavior is "reinforced" with a reward, it will become more likely to occur in the future.

Neuroscientists have discovered the mechanisms by which this system is implemented in the brain. Upon satisfaction of one of these basic needs—such as being hungry and eating a big juicy steak—systems involved in processing reward and excitement flood the brain with neurochemicals like endorphins and dopamine.

These stimulate a feeling of intense exhilaration and excitement. At the same time, neuromodulators like acetylcholine are released by areas of the brain responsible for forming memories. These chemicals switch the brain over to "storage" mode, causing rapid and long-lasting impressions to form.

Every detail of the experience leading to the satisfaction of these urges is powerfully etched into our neurons, and so every detail of a successful hunt would be permanently associated with that powerful feeling of exhilaration.

Mammals have a specific reward site in the brain called the nucleus accumbens, which signals happiness and satisfaction after a successful event. This became active in our ancestors' brains after the discovery of a rich honeycomb or the end of a successful hunt.

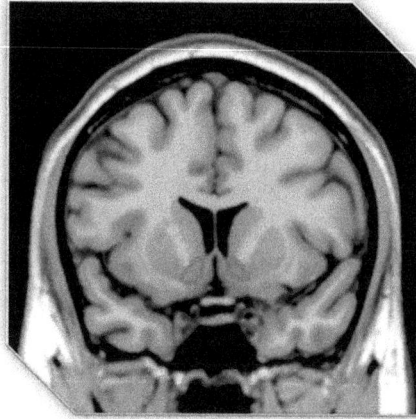

Location of the nucleus accumbens

This is the same brain area responsible for giving addicted gamblers a "hit" when they contemplate winning, one almost as powerful as that from cocaine. The same area lights up during a PET scan when an investor contemplates a financial gain.[2]

A groundbreaking book, Your Money and Your Brain by Jason Zweig, explains that we become addicted to and crave gain, sometimes more than life itself.

This system worked well for our ancestors, and may work well for the Hazda on the Serengeti. If we change even one variable, we can upset the balance on which it depends. For example, as hunting technology improved even slightly with the onset of longer spears and more powerful spear-throwing devices such as the atlatl, humans became even more voracious hunters.

Whereas it was once an almost impossible task to take down big game, the introduction of a simple technology—a notched piece of wood into which the spear shaft could rest —allowed our ancestors to hurl heavy spears with over 200 times as much power and at 6 times the range. (Incidentally, the world record for an atlatl throw is a staggering 848.56 feet, set by Dave Ingvall of Missouri on July 15, 1995.)

This innovation allowed humans to penetrate the thick hides of mammoth and wooly rhinoceros from a safe distance, and so began a great, centuries-long feast. As a result, popular theories today suggest that much of the world's big game was hunted to extinction by mankind as little as 10,000 years ago. In turn, many northern populations of humans were themselves pushed to the brink of extermination by the resultant lack of food.

How could our ancestors not realize the danger of their overconsumption? What was going through the mind of the hunter that killed the last wooly mammoth? The answer, as we'll see, is that their behavioral programming did not have time to catch up to how the new technology changed their relationship with the environment.

Atlatl

Many men who have accumulated more millions of money than they can ever use have shown a rabid hunger for more, and have not scrupled to cheat the ignorant and the helpless out of their poor servings in order to partially appease that appetite. I furnished a hundred different kinds of wild and tame animals the opportunity to accumulate vast stores of food, but none of them would do it.
Mark Twain

Something as simple as an atlatl threw humanity off-balance. Imagine what the supremely unnatural environments created by modern technology and the 24-hour news cycle can do to a poor pauper's brain. One of the first problems was caused by something we nowadays take for granted: currency.

Money in itself doesn't satisfy any basic needs. It doesn't taste good and mating with it is out of the question. But money can buy access to primary reinforcers. Through this association, money becomes what psychologists call a secondary reinforcer.

This means that while money can have the same emotional significance as food and sex. Money doesn't have the natural "stopping signals" as primary reinforcers. We can now recognize the danger.

When munching on the group kill, our ancestors would eventually feel fullness in their bellies, telling them to stop eating. When collecting stone tools, our ancestors would eventually amass a load too heavy to move when their troop struck camp and moved to better foraging grounds.

Money, on the other hand, is different because it comes with no natural stopping signals. Linked to a lightweight checkbook, ATM, or credit card, we can carry as much of it as we want; and with sufficient credit, the sky's the limit. With no natural stopping signals to tell us that we have enough, we continually want more and more of it.

Knowing that paupers have these shortcomings, other humans create environments to take advantage of them. Consider one of the pauper's most notorious foraging environments, casinos. These unnatural environments are specifically engineered by gambling experts. Psychologists and neuroscientists have developed strategies to extract the maximum amount of money from paupers in casinos. The strategies hit all the right pleasure points in the pauper brains.

Another robust finding in psychology is called the principle of differential reinforcement. In the 1950s, reinforcement learning was all the rage in American psychology and psychologists like B. F. Skinner conducted thousands of experiments on reinforcement learning.

Their goal was to predict, with mathematical precision, how much of a reward would be required to get rats, pigeons, and eventually humans to perform specific kinds of behavior.

Their experiments were wildly successful. For the first time in history, we seemed able to mathematically calculate when an organism would engage in a certain behavior. The results were based on knowledge of how often that behavior was rewarded in the past.

Now you might think that the most effective schedule was to reward critters every time they performed the desired behavior. But a surprising finding that arose in this research was that the "always win" reward schedule was not the most effective.

Rather, Skinner and others found that a "variable ratio" schedule, where only an occasional big reward was received, was most effective in producing the desired behavior.

Neuroscientists have since learned the neural explanation for this is that receiving a large number of rewards in a short period of time depletes the brain's pleasure-inducing dopamine reserves. It also wears out the areas of the brain that receive dopamine, causing them to become less receptive. In short, the pleasure centers of the brain get tired and bored when they receive too much pleasure too quickly.

An occasional big success bookended by a large amount of monotonous failure seems to provide the brain with just the right mix of rest and reward. Sound like a one-armed bandit to you?

The modern casino experience is nothing but hunting and foraging on steroids. Look at the images depicted on slot machines, particularly those related to big payouts. Many involve pictures of things our ancestors desired, such as treasure, beautiful women or animals.

Cognitive Dissonance

When the reward system of the brain takes over, people become uncharacteristically brave. Contemplating the possibility of a "big score," they lose sight of danger and risk. I've seen periods of collective insanity. Almost everyone started investing in the same thing.

People would discard their balanced portfolios and load up with tech stocks, hedge funds, or gold as if there was no tomorrow. I've heard investors repeat catch phases from financial advertisements that support their impulsive actions. Sane people not caught in the mania might conclude these investors were caught in a bubble and future gains would not continue.

In hindsight, the tech bubble of the late 1990s made no sense. How could P/E ratios[3] of 200 and more be sustainable? Financial analysts predicted the growth of sales would sustain such high multiples. While technology has transformed our lives as was widely predicted, many of the startup companies that flourished during the tech bubble don't exist today.

Companies that had never made a profit were selling for absurd prices. Financial advisors knew it was an official bubble when the smallest investors craved stocks they'd never heard of before, such as Cisco, Yahoo and Worldcom, despite having no idea what those companies did.

The Nasdaq index soared to all-time highs in March of 2000, topping 5,000. Ten years later, in March of 2010, the fabled index stood at less than half of that number. During this investment bubble, a few of my clients questioned why I had not loaded up their portfolios with the high-tech stocks that were driving the bubble.

They were fully prepared to abandon the balanced portfolios that delivered lower returns while protecting against the occasional selloff. They envied the returns some of their neighbors were getting with high tech stocks and wanted to share the bounty.

Sensing this greed, predatory marketers in the guise of financial advisors and investment industry analysts convinced investors to load up on the next "hot dot." They persuaded investors to churn their own accounts!

Like carnival barkers, financial pitchmen know how human instincts work and do not hesitate to take advantage of that knowledge. Fortunes have been made by providing deceptively attractive investment products the masses want to buy.

This is one reason our investment system is broken. People convince themselves they will be rich. Their brains flood their bodies with endorphins and other feel-good chemicals.[4] The "highs" not only numb them to information that should make them wary but are so powerful that investors will do almost anything to experience them again.

These powerful chemicals and those that come from overwhelming fear trigger behavioral biases in most investors. It's out of our control. The brain is on chemical overload.

In the face of opposing facts that would prompt caution and dissuade investors from their precipitous course, they instead allow themselves to be led into the sea like lemmings. The result is almost certain financial doom. Not only do people fall for it once; but unless the cycle is broken, they will continue to do so.

When investors get a "hit" of unusual success—as raw luck will occasionally grant anyone—they are imprinted to attempt to repeat the same success. This is reminiscent of the prospector who finds one big gold nugget and spends the rest of his life searching for the mother lode until he has wasted his last cent. Those who chase every technology startup are no different from the old prospector: they are attempting to repeat their earlier successes.

There are other behaviors and biases related to greed, such as hoarding, herding, denial of loss and collecting behaviors that can also influence investment decisions, often to our detriment. We'll discuss them in later chapters.

Whenever irrational exuberance appears, you can bet another bubble has formed, and every bubble is caused by greed. At the moment of decision, stock market and bond investors have clouded judgment when motivated by greed. With practice, investors can learn to recognize this gambling behavior in others and avoid investing in overpriced stocks.

It's not always easy to tell when irrational exuberance[5] has taken hold. When it occurs, nearly everyone is infected by the mania, so you certainly can't rely on your neighbors or even your advisors, in some cases. I like to use the Duck Test to judge whether a moment in time might be one of irrational exuberance:

If it waddles like a duck, quacks like a duck, and lays eggs like a duck, it's probably a duck.

What does irrational exuberance quack like?

- Everyone is talking about it.

- Every other advertisement is about it.

- People say, "But this time it is different."

- Small investors are buying it. Hedge funds are buying it. Everybody is buying it.

- Investors are likely to be buying it on margin or some other type of leveraged purchase.

- Analysts are upbeat about the future of it. There are usually record numbers of investment strategies introduced featuring it.

- Many investors put all their money into it because "it's such a great investment, it has to go up."

- Con artists start selling it.

If it's quacking, don't invest in it. If your advisor recommends it, fire him or her.

Chapter Two

Fight or Flight

*If you want to test your memory, try to recall what
you were worrying about one year ago today.*
E. Joseph Cossman

The ancient world was a dangerous place. Around every turn, ferocious animals hunted our early relatives. There were times of feast and famine. Other tribes tried to steal resources. Our ancient family members constantly coped with threats and failure.

To survive, our brave ancestors had to recognize the dangers of their surroundings quickly. They would have only seconds to detect a lion leaping from the bushes or an enemy war party sneaking into camp.

Our 21st century brains have the same danger-sensing mechanisms as those of our forefathers. When we anticipate peril, our brains burst into action in what is called the fight or flight response. The same basic mechanisms cause our 21st-century bodies to respond to the brain's signals by preparing us for battle or retreat.

The core of the fight or flight response is the preparation for physical action. Our autonomic nervous system is the part of the brain and spinal cord responsible for regulating all the automatic stuff. You never think about functions such as breathing, heartbeat, and digestion. The ANS is divided into two main components:

- The parasympathetic nervous system (PNS), also known as the "rest and digest" part of the system, acts to grow and maintain the body at rest.

- The sympathetic nervous system (SNS) rapidly mobilizes and transports energy to the muscles so they are ready for extreme bursts of action.

Our fight or flight response is triggered when our SNS detects a dangerous situation. When it snaps into action, it causes the endocrine system—the network of glands and organs responsible for regulating our hormones—to flood our bodies with a complex symphony of chemicals. These include epinephrine, norepine-phrine, glucocorticoids (a kind of steroid, including cortisol), endorphins, and vasopressin, each with a different purpose.

Epinephrine (adrenaline) and norepinephrine increase breathing and heartbeat, focus attention and increase our perceptual acuity. Glucocorticoids turn off the immune system (to save energy), enhance memory and increase the conversion of fat into blood sugar to provide fuel for the muscles.

Endorphins deaden us to the sensation of pain, allowing us to continue fighting or fleeing even when injured. Vasopressin dilates the blood vessels, helping us retain water and slow bleeding.

PNS releases its own symphony of chemicals that often does just the reverse: they increase the conversion of blood sugar into fat, stimulate digestion, move blood flow from the limbs to the gut, decrease awareness and anxiety, and make us feel tired. Melatonin is a good example and regulates the circadian sleep cycles of the body.

When the two systems work in balance, it's a wonder to behold. We respond to dangers with maximum efficiency when they occur. We calmly store away energy in the off periods to prepare for the next call to action.

Indeed, one can view everything in nature as the old dilemma of investment. A bear lays on layers of fat in preparation for hibernation; the snowshoe hare spends its energy growing a thick winter coat; they are both choosing the slow and steady course for long-term success rather than expending the resources on bursts of enjoyment.

The Ant and The Grasshopper

You may recall Aesop's fable about the ant and the grasshopper wherein the grasshopper spends the warm summer months singing and dancing in the grass, enjoying the plenty. Meanwhile the ant spends the summer meticulously storing away food for winter. When winter arrives, the grasshopper is left starving and comes begging to the ant for help.

In this scientific tale, the PNS is the ant and the SNS is the grasshopper. PNS prepares us for digestion and rest while SNS mobilizes resources for physical action, preparing us for emergencies.

SNS is specialized for less-efficient, high-intensity, short-term action useful in a crisis. It heightens our senses, dilating our pupils and focusing our attention on even the most minute sounds or tactile sensations. It accelerates our heartbeats, increasing the flow of blood and oxygen to our muscles.

SNS causes some physical changes that make a bit less sense and are often significantly less convenient. It triggers goose bumps (piloerection), inhibits digestion, decreases saliva and can even cause the bowels to release. Some of these changes make sense from an evolutionary perspective. Goosebumps might make human skin look weird and feel uncomfortable. The same reaction made our hairier mammalian ancestors' fur stand on end, making them look much larger and more intimidating to predators.

When these two systems operate in balance, everything works remarkably well. We remain fit, healthy, happy, fed, rested and ready for action. If the grasshopper throws too many parties, however, soon the ant doesn't have any extra food left to give him.

This is the fate of the chronically stressed-out person who, unable to sleep or eat, falls into illness.

Contrary to Aesop, an overabundance of the ant's behavior can be just as detrimental. All rest and no play are not any fun either. It leaves us fat, slow, sleepy and depressed. Worse, modern life can leave us both stressed and exhausted, causing both the SNS and PNS to be active simultaneously.

Piloerection in a cat

This is a perilous situation for the body. According to leading stress researcher Robert Sapolsky, it is akin to slamming your foot on both the gas pedal and the brakes at the same time—bad for both the engine and the brakes.[6]

The problem with our fight or flight response is that while it is brilliantly adapted to deal with short-term physical crises, it's not so good at dealing with the kinds of psychological, professional, and financial crises we face in modern life. The emergencies faced by our ancestors were over quickly. The troop offered an unambiguous "all clear!" signals that our body could use to switch off the SNS.

A wildebeest attacked by a lion experiences a crisis that ends quickly: it gets eaten or it escapes. The body can end the stress response when one of these two outcomes occurs. Modern emergencies can be similar, and sometimes we get lucky.

If you are about to miss your flight, the fight or flight (pun intended) response might be just what the doctor ordered. On short notice, it can help you race through the terminal, baggage in tow, avoid collisions with other travelers, and find your gate. The crisis ends, and the stress response can be switched off when you either board your flight or miss it.

Unfortunately for our health and our investments, modern stressors can persist over long periods of time, surrounding us with terrors real and imagined, with no end in sight. You hear a company rumor that layoffs are imminent; you may live for months, without relief, under the fear of losing your job. The nightly news drums up fear about the latest recession, Covid variant or war.

Reports of rising crime rates and gun violence can leave you afraid to leave home. Inflation fears and gas prices can stress anyone. And don't even get started on election prognostications that certain doom will befall the country should the other side win.

Unlike the situations faced by our ancestors, rumored layoffs, lethal viruses, recessions and criminals lurking in the dark are nebulous and unseen dangers. The perceived threats persist for as long as we think about them, although no immediate danger is present. And while the stressful situations eventually end—your job is spared and the flu or Covid season passes without illness— they persist far longer than your bodies and minds were built to sustain.

Viewed from the perspective of the evolution of the animal kingdom, sustained psychological stress is a recent invention, mostly limited to humans and other social primates.
Robert Sapolsky

Bottom Sellers

Recall our pauper who has just received his quarterly investment statement reporting a big loss. This will surely set off his SNS, mobilizing a quick burst of resources to allow him to either run like hell or respond with a quick and vicious counterattack. If these were the proper responses, the system would be well designed for the task.

Unfortunately, it's not well designed to help make sound financial decisions. It was never meant for constant chronic use, which results in what we now call stress. In other words, you won't have a very enjoyable or quality life if your body is constantly responding to financial reports as though they were charging lions.

The 21st century investor that contemplates loss can feel the same emotions as our ancestors felt when attacked by wild animals. Our fight or flight reflex[7] kicks into high gear, and we must fight or flee danger at all cost.

Unless someone is continually overcome by negative news, fight or flight tends to be a short- lived sensation. An investor experiencing a deluge of bad news might suffer the same dread, depression, headache, stomachache and insomnia as our ancient forefathers did when facing mortal danger. And while the threat would likely have been over quickly for our ancestors, today's investor isn't as fortunate.

This is one reason why modern investors end up grasping for artificial stopping signals, even when they know it's the irrational thing to do. They demand to sell out at the market bottom and lock in their losses, just to bring resolution to the horrible stress response that is robbing them of their quality of life.

If you are distressed by anything external, the pain is not due to the thing itself, but to your estimate of it; and this you have the power to revoke at any moment.
Marcus Aurelius

Emergency Life Stage Reaction

Another advanced stage of contemplating substantial loss could cause an investor to enter into the emergency life stage[8] reaction. A common symptom of this crossover is the inability to stop thinking about loss combined with overwhelming repetitive negativity. The victim continually scours for updates on the situation.

The mass media and internet—seeking to maximize ad revenue by increasing audience participation—are willing accomplices, providing investors with a constant stream of increasingly dire (and often overhyped) news during a downturn.

It's no surprise that all this can make a modern investor clinically neurotic. And it isn't all in the investor's head. It's a very real reaction affecting most of the body, and the natural result of constant fear that possibly saved our ancestors from being killed or eaten. Having the fight or flight reaction is natural and even healthy in some circumstances. The crossover into the emergency life stage reaction isn't healthy for investors or their investment decisions.

Behavioral Finance has researched biases that affect investor judgement. If an investor is ill, they sell their investments more often. If an investor's stomach feels off, they sell their investments more often. Logic and sound investing have less to do with the decision than how you feel.

Moreover, some people are more susceptible to adverse reactions than others. Investors who inherit a triple dose of the reaction might be compelled to sell out at the bottom of a market cycle. Look at a graph of any stock as it reached its lowest price; that dip marks a day when millions of investors sold, despite the fact they likely knew to sell high and buy low.

Market bottoms are often reached on a record volume day as a result of investors selling at exactly the wrong time, the precise time when they should be buying like crazy in order to buy at the low and make a profit. A market bottom by definition is when there is zero risk stocks will go lower.

The investors that sell out at the bottom lock in the loss, sometimes for life. From a wealth perspective, selling out at the bottom is the most damaging action investors can take. Those investors that simply ignore the bad news are likely to retain their investments and see the dog of the day become the next high-flying stock.

Let's apply the Duck Test again, to help ensure you never sell at the bottom.

1. Your fellow worker, neighbor or brother-in-law advised you to sell because they just did.

2. Your local paper prints a graph of the stock market on the front page and warns that it's going lower.

3. Twitter, Facebook and even investment publications say it's never been this bad and it's going to get worse.

4. The analysts predict things will get worse.

5. Dire predictions abound. Many sources advise an immediate switch to cash.

6. Organizations like Occupy Wallstreet are formed to fight or protest. Maybe even a political movement is formed, new laws are passed, books are written and specials are run on television.

The folks that freeze may simply stop reading their statements. Their buy and hold strategy can be the least damaging reaction to have, particularly during a severe downturn.

As an investor, you should know who you are before making investment decisions. Consider whether you are prone to fight or flight reactions, or better, discuss the possibility with a qualified investment professional first.

Failure to do so could result in costly impulsive reactions in response to a significant drop in portfolio value. Some knowledge of investor psychology, behavioral finance priciples and market history can help avoid panic at the bottom of a market cycle. What goes down can and often does go back up if left alone.

Knowing that today's investor is prone to panic could be a valuable piece of information. Pervasive negative news makes it more likely investors will transition from the normal fight or flight reaction to the more serious emergency life stage reaction. Some investors could progress to clinical depression or financial post-traumatic stress disorder. People really did jump from windows on Wall Street during the 1929 market crash.

Recently the S&P 500, a stock index of the 500 largest companies in the United States, returned a jaw dropping 24% return in just 90 days. April 1, 2020 the index stood at 2,498.08 and ended at 3,105.92 on July 1, 2020. Numerous studies show that the best index results often come after a bear market selloff.

You must be invested to get the best days, weeks and months gains in the stock market. The index dropped a gut churning 16% during the month of March 2020.

More recently the Nasdaq, an American stock exchange based in New York and ranked second behind the New York Stock Exchange, lost over 34 percent from its high in November 2021, and might even go lower.

For the panicked investor, these are trying times. But for every seller there is another investor that's buying. When the recession is over the buyers will be the ones getting the best returns.

The brave wise souls who stayed the course with solid, balanced portfolios more than recovered and now have healthy gains. The paupers who sold out at the bottom locked in their losses. The wise investors who invested new cash on April 1, 2020 are well on their way to becoming rich. The future is yet to be revealed.

On Impatience

Mankind hasn't always been as successful as our species is today. Our ancient ancestors often faced extinction. Over millions of years of evolution, we developed skills to assess situations almost instantly. Those skills and their study are called heuristics.

Heuristics allow us to make swift decisions with minimal information. Modern computers can perform billions of mathematical calculations per second but struggle with making simple decisions in rushed or uncertain conditions. Man's modern mind operates identically to that of its ancient ancestors when it comes to making fast, accurate decisions with limited information.

Let's speculate how ancient man perceived his environment. Every sense would have alerted our ancient relatives to danger, opportunity, and the social workings of the troop. If a tiger or lion approached, they would quickly react and run to safety.

Had they not, they would have died before passing on their genes. Our prehistoric ancestors couldn't defeat a predator with teeth or fists, nor could they outrun them. They avoided extinction by thinking faster and more accurately than other wilderness animals. The oft-repeated truism "Your first choice is usually the most accurate" may be more accurate than anyone suspected.

Modern men and women make split-second decisions on investments that might or might not be accurate. The problem is that hucksters and salesmen know how to take advantage of our heuristics.

Given that investors are likely to become enamored with a company or stock if characterized by certain attributes, they are forever vulnerable to the pump and dump, "story" stocks and Ponzi schemes that tout investments that are less than solid.

Bernard L. "Bernie" Madoff ran the largest known Ponzi scheme, starting in the 1960's. Bernie's firm was exclusive. The wealthy lined up to buy what Bernie was selling. His statements were spectacular: clients averaged 15 percent annually and never suffered a down year.

He could look a client in the eye and lie. His heuristics were impeccable. Victims reported they would plead with Bernie to take their money. When his sons alerted authorities that something was amiss on December 11, 2008, liabilities of the firm were estimated to be around $50 billion.

I wish that Bernie's story was unusual but it's not. Most towns have someone like Bernie that you instinctively trust, perhaps a member of your church. He or she promises a guaranteed return.

"I may not make you rich, but I guarantee not to make you poor" was the slogan of a local Ponzi schemer that guaranteed 12 percent a year when banks were paying 4 percent. The fact that Ponzi schemers will likely spend the rest of their lives in prison does little good for the victims.

How a story is presented can strongly influence an investor's instant decisions. They regularly embrace the "can't miss" promise of the con artist while ignoring the reasoned approach of the honest investment advisor. The adage you've heard a hundred times—if it's too good to be true, it probably is—bears repeating yet again.

Predators masquerading as advisors and wealth managers flourish in the 21st-century investment jungle. Their advantage over the predators we evolved to avoid is that they know how to exploit the blind spots in our brains.

One successful ruse is to show glowing but fraudulent past performance or to promise bogus guarantees. That's how Bernie Madoff did it.

Let's apply the Duck Test. What do con artists or Ponzi schemers look like? Here are a few examples:

1. They will promise you an exceptional rate of return.

2. They will appear trustworthy and prosperous.

3. They lie easily, without flinching.

4. They promise a guarantee not being offered by others for similar investments.

5. People you trust have bought in, based on endorsements and testimonials.

6. They are apt to use your church or synagogue as a marketing venue. Bernie was Jewish and sold mainly to investors in his faith. He frequently used faith to close the deal. Most professionals don't market through the church.

7. They give evasive answers. When asked if the investment is liquid, they respond, "You can get 10 percent a year without a penalty." Translation: It's illiquid. 90 percent is tied up for a very long time.

8. They advertise heavily.

There are many ways investors let their emotions run away with them. Any time someone gets emotional about an investment, they are likely to be damaged by poor decisions. If you are especially emotional about an investment, it may be best to delay your decision.

I caution that that is likely true when you are selling after a market downturn or buying after a market upturn. You might return to the Introduction and review APT decision-making: Acknowledge, Pause and Think. Just knowing that there are some very powerful chemicals coursing through your body and brain should give you Pause.

During periods of extreme market volatility, I constantly remind my clients that their investments are of good quality and are helping them meet their goals by paying a reasonable dividend, interest, or growing at a reasonable rate. Their investment incomes likely haven't decreased, and it's highly unlikely that the world is not coming to an end.

A similar theme that often will allow an investor to relax follows the buy and hold advice. "Your account will likely be higher a year from now." If the economy is in a crisis, a year from now the crisis will be over, the election will be decided and uncertainty will not be a problem for investors.

Similarly, I might have to advise them that the new "golden investment" they heard about might come with more risk than their current portfolio—even though the advertising states "returns have doubled in the last decade."

It's hard for many investors to believe that advertisers or marketers can be deceptive. When someone believes, they are going to make a phenomenal profit on an investment, such as the

Iraqi Dinar Scam that continues to circulate, the chemicals explode in their brain.

This explosion borders on a hit from a powerful drug. I am forced to bring them back to reality. I help them APT or pause and reflect.

Security regulators including FINRA® and The Securities and Exchange Commission often issue cease and desist orders. Marketers convince investors to sell their solid stock market-based investments. "Stocks are too risky" or "will become worthless" during the next crash and buy whatever they are selling.

Bitcoin, gold coins, oil and gas investments and penny stocks are frequently portrayed as safe. What the sellers and vendors of those investments won't tell you is there's a 25% commission for the fraudster or that the digital currency account doesn't really exist.

The most vulnerable are the young and the old investor. Senior investors are the most targeted because they have the money and they might have lost mental capacity to make decisions. GenXers and millennials are targeted because they lack experience and are likely to want the quick riches promised by fraudsters.

FINRA® and SEC are issuing regulation after regulation that attempts to reduce the abuse and fraud. Advisors are being educated every year on how to recognize elder abuse, money laundering, scams and identity theft. It's your responsibility to reduce your own chances of being a victim.

Chapter Three

Predictions

Whether trying to predict patterns in our environment or patterns in the prices of stocks, our 21st century brains and those of our ancient ancestors work the same way. Our ancient ancestors could calculate a bird's flight path, its future location and the speed and trajectory of an arrow.

With practice, they could shoot dinner right out of the sky. They also had to predict the changing seasons and weather patterns and prepare accordingly. Our brains are the most advanced and efficient prediction devices in the world.

Today, we often use our brain's prediction capability when playing games. There are golfers who can hit a ball 200-plus yards and stop it just inches from the hole. Consider the skill of a fisherman who can land a dry fly upstream into a trout hole with no drag on the line so that a fish rises up and takes the artificial bait. You may not possess these skills but your mind is capable of the actions.

We are all just a bunch of hunter-gatherers. Look at baseball. It's just a rock and a stick. Hockey is a rock, a stick and a fight. Golf is a rock, a stick and a hole in the ground.
Alan Parisse

Our incessant drive to predict, however, has a dark side. We 21st century humans are hard-wired to try to find patterns in every source of information. We often think we see a pattern when none exists. It's a holdover from ancient times when continuing cycles were evident. Birds continued their predictable flight paths; seasons repeated themselves year after year.

The ancient world was more predictable. Today's world events involve increasingly complex economic and political interactions not dependent upon natural cycles. Unlike modern man, our ancient family members didn't instantaneously hear about earthquakes or famines on the other side of the planet. Today, we must endure the minute-by-minute speculative commentary of hundreds of well-meaning pundits, and bad news will always dominate the headlines.

Water flowed predictably from the creek near our ancestor's cave, but can we assume dividends will flow forever from oil or bank stocks? Will the Dow Jones Industrial Average[9] (DJIA) continue in the same direction month after month, year after year? Will that tech stock continue to rise?

Historical evidence tells us these assumptions are obviously false, yet we still get suckered into believing them. We trust that gold or real estate will continually go up—or down—depending on where the markets find themselves at the time.

The problem is that the financial markets never seem aligned with the predictable seasonal cycles that confronted our ancestors. As a result, we keep trying to force the evidence to fit simple, understandable patterns.

Our 21st Century world is anything but predictable; stock market predictability is even more elusive. The movement of stock prices on a daily basis is quite random[10], yet day-trading investors spend fortunes on software that purports to predict a pattern. Our instincts tell us that if we gather enough information about a stock or investment we want to buy or sell, success is assured.

While there are patterns, the movements of markets and investments remain unpredictable. The pauper brain, however, continues to make predictions. Some might even make intuitive sense, but again, intuition can betray the investor.

For example, when the threat of war occurs, the stock market is likely to react to the uncertainty by going down. There is no certainty, but the mere prospect of war is sufficient to derail the stock market. The stock market hates uncertainty. Stocks trade down because of uncertainty. If war is declared and the fighting begins, the resulting certainty typically triggers a rally.

The stock market likes war. The armed forces buy weapons and blow things up. Companies make profits supplying arms, ammunition, weaponry and other tools of conflict. Employment soars. Money flows. Aside from the loss of life, it's likely a reliable way to stimulate the economy.

So when war comes, it's a good time to buy stocks, right? Well, that depends on what type of stocks. The best time to buy defense industry stocks is when there is no talk or contemplation of war because that's when prices and profits are the lowest. Similarly, the best time to buy gold is when economic uncertainty is low.

Conversely, defense stocks might be sold when war is declared and fighting starts, or most certainly before peace is declared. A good time to sell gold is likely when economic uncertainty is highest. The future is yet to be written but in the past, this pattern has been proven to be true.

Why is this so often the case?

Because paupers buy gold when economic uncertainty is at its peak. They buy defense stocks when war is anticipated, declared, and when peace is restored. Of course, that's when the prices are typically higher. Paupers pay high prices for everything. Those who sell at high prices to paupers make high profits. You want to sell your inflated stuff to paupers at high prices? To do this, you need a plan.

Bonds behave somewhat differently. High-quality, long-duration bonds often gain value when interest rates on similar new-issue bonds fall. The time to buy high-quality, long-duration bonds is often when interest rates have risen. The time to sell is after interest rates have fallen. It's difficult to tell when interest rates will cause problems.

Highest-quality bonds generally offer a risk-free return if held to maturity. Paupers buy short certificates of deposit that offer higher interest rates late in a boom cycle—just when they should be buying long-duration, high-quality bonds.

Now that we have the playing field defined, let's discuss whether you are comfortable buying and selling investments because you intuitively feel they should, could, might or must go up or down in value.

Analysts are often baffled by why things happen. The solution may be to ignore the analysts. Stop trying to predict what will happen. In the following chapters, I'll discuss how to create a balanced portfolio that will help you overcome the urge to predict the markets.

Here's the most difficult transition I make in this book. Trading using your gut or intuition is the least successful trading strategy. Knowing where we are in the economic cycle is very necessary. Owning appropriate stocks and bonds for the current economic situation is worth 100 times the price of this book.

There's a saying that each day in the stock market is a "random walk" for investors. Each day has its own reasons for the trades that occur. I believe that each trading market has its own cycle that occurs repeatedly. There are predictable patterns that emerge time and time again.

There are cycles of various lengths, but I am going to focus on the one- and four- to-eight-year cycles. These are the most predictable and tradable cycles, called the Bust and Boom cycle and the Sell in May and Go Away and Year-End Rally cycle.

The Bust and Boom cycle is caused by the Federal Reserve Board's monetary policy and world and national economic trends. The Sell in May and Go Away and Year-End Rally cycle is caused by annual recurring investor behavior.

For paupers, it's a flip of the coin as to how they might interpret the data. I don't recommend trying to understand how each cycle works unless you are trained in economic studies. Frankly, you might be better off to just flip a coin than let your intuition and instincts rule how you invest.

This is going to get interesting and fun. Stick with it. This is where you will really have a basis to buy the appropriately balanced portfolio for the economic moment in time we find today.

The Boom Bust Cycle

The boom bust cycle (or business cycle) is caused by normal business expansions and contractions. Economic theory states that during slow economic activity or recession, interest rates will usually be lower due to less demand for lending.

When interest rates are lower, businesses will borrow money and expand. When businesses expand, they order more goods, which stimulates other businesses to expand.

Prices rise as demand for goods, services and labor rise. Businesses hire more workers during the expansion, and consequently unemployment drops. Fewer workers are available in the unemployed labor pool.

In some instances, employers begin a bidding war for workers, resulting in higher salaries. Unions negotiate for ever-increasing salaries.

In this economic environment, optimism rules the day. Tax revenues rise, and governments commit to supplying more services and hiring more workers, thus fueling another rise in overall labor costs. Commodity prices often rise as well.

Prices for goods, services, and labor all spiral upward until inflation begins to erode the purchasing power of the consumer. This prompts intervention by the Federal Reserve Board (FED), which raises short-term interest rates. Often the short-term interest rates are higher than long-term interest rates because businesses aren't borrowing anymore.

An inverted or flat yield curve—signaled by long-term interest rates being lower than short-term interest rates—can occur, further confusing business owners, consumers and investors. The stock market reaches a new high. Wise investors sell stocks and invest in high quality long-term debt.

The cost to borrow goes up; the cost of goods goes up. This makes businesses less profitable. Businesses begin to lose faith in the expansion. Businesses and consumers buy less. Profits fall, and eventually, losses begin to appear on balance sheets.

Governments start to collect less revenue and are unable to provide all the promised services. Most businesses and governments begin to lay off employees. A contraction has begun to take hold of the economy.

Unemployment rises. Confidence erodes. Businesses begin to feel a crunch from lenders. Debt is often called, or interest rates for those with lower credit go higher.

Businesses can find themselves in default of debt or must take drastic measures to raise funds by selling hard assets like real estate to remain solvent. There's too much real estate on the market and not enough buyers. Real estate prices fall.

The FED lowers short-term interest rates. This continues for months and sometimes years, putting liquidity into the market and making businesses more profitable. Businesses and governments are in full contraction and cut back on inventory, labor costs, supplies, and purchases of every sort.

Profits are low. Losses rise. Consumers worry the economy will not recover. The FED continues to lower interest rates and use every trick in the book and sometimes not in the book to stimulate the economy.

Unemployment tops out at a ghastly high figure and is predicted to go even higher. The FED lowers the short-term interest to record low rates.

Consumers panic. Pauper investors sell their investments at rock bottom prices. Businesses go bankrupt. Banks fail and are taken over by FDIC.

Meanwhile, knowledgeable investors buy stock and real estate investments with solid fundamentals during the selloff. Pauper investors buy certificates of deposits at unheard of low interest rates, tying their money up...sometimes for years.

Once the system has wrung every last quality investment out of the paupers, the bottom is declared, and the recovery begins.

Unemployment, a lagging indicator, usually peaks months later. Paupers think unemployment is bad for businesses and profits, but all it means is that businesses have affordable labor and reduced costs. Profits start to rise, and the stock market is well into the next cycle's rally.

Stock prices rise, indicating that wise investors anticipate a recovery. Stimuli by the FED takes anywhere from six to eighteen months to take effect. Wise investors buy before the bottom of the recession.

How do they know? The moment the FED raises short-term interest rates, wise investors anticipate recession, sell stocks and buy high quality AAA bonds.

This cycle historically has averaged five years but can be shorter or longer. The contraction phase to the bottom of the recession averages about a year, and the expansion boom to the contraction phase averages four years.

Longer expansions are signaled by slow growth, low interest rates and higher unemployment. Shorter expansions are signaled by rapid growth, low unemployment and higher inflation rates.

Stock Market Reaction to Business Cycles

There are two inflection points when wise investors make changes in their balanced portfolios. The first, point A, is when wise investors begin to take certain classes of investments that lose value during contraction off the table and buy investments that appreciate during a contraction and recession.

Point A is characterized by the FED tightening credit. Businesses and stocks are strong. The yield curve[11] is stable but beginning to flatten.

Institutional investors sense the slowdown is coming and begin investing in longer-duration bonds. Businesses are buying materials and building inventories aggressively.

Employment is stable but it's getting difficult and costly to hire. Astute businesses slow down hiring and growth. Credit is abundant and cheap. Consumer sentiment is high. Inflation is accelerating.

Over the following months, wise investors set in motion a plan to:

- Harvest gains from low-credit quality bonds that have rallied during the strong economy; reduce exposure to junk and lower-grade corporate bonds.

- Increase bond portfolio quality by buying Treasuries AAA agency bonds, AAA CMOs and highest-grade municipal bonds.

- Reduce the duration or sell low-quality debt and increase the duration on high-quality debt.

- Monitor equity volatility. As it increases, you should begin to rotate from growth investments to materials, energy, healthcare, pharmaceuticals and large-cap, dividend-paying stocks.

- Avoid being fooled by elevated short-term yields. Short certificates of deposit are likely to be paying great rates, but the storm is coming. Long bonds might be yielding even less, called a reverse yield curve— often thought to be a signal that recession is around the corner Paupers will be rolling 90-day CDs, thinking that interest rates will continue to rise.

- Be cautious about going into debt. Begin to build some cash.

- Slow contributions to retirement plans and get ready to make "get-conservative" 401k changes. Make similar changes to your IRA's, Roth's and individual accounts. Put stops on stock positions to reduce losses during the volatile market selloff that is likely to happen. The most sophisticated investors will buy puts or protective options.[12]

Point B is characterized by a weak economy. The yield curve continues to steepen. Long interest rates may be at their lowest due to low demand and pervasive pessimism.

The FED lowers rates and may be stimulating the economy with quantitative easing tactics[13]. Economists are not as concerned about inflation, which inflation appears to be worrisome in a few sectors of the economy. Credit is tight. Volatility soars.

Corporate high-yielding or junk bonds often trade more like stocks and are in full correction mode, irrationally selling below their intrinsic values and offering attractive, high annual yields.

Equities are also in full correction mode with panic setting in. While economists have not yet declared a recession, they are speculating about the possibility.

Institutional investors sense a change and begin to shorten durations on bond investments. A wall of worry grips the nation. The private sector lays off workers. Municipalities experience revenue decreases, and municipal defaults are rumored.

Wise investors begin to make changes in their portfolio:

- The best buys in equities are likely to be financials, technology, transportation and small cap stocks, where appropriate.

- Emerging market stocks may be depressed, offering attractive buys.

- Begin to sell high-grade bonds to lock in gains. Increase credit risk and begin to nibble at high-yield bonds. As the recession deepens, concentrate on lower-quality bonds, where appropriate.

- Harvest gains from long-duration bonds; avoid callable bonds.

- Anticipating recession being declared and the FED increasing stimulation, aggressive investors increase debt.

- As the Fed continues its ineffective stimulation, sell off the most conservative positions and invest at the aggressive end of the balanced portfolio.

- Real estate is often a bargain at this stage. Buy with both hands if offered at distressed prices and attractive yields. Be picky. Better prices may be available a bit later in the cycle as banks are taken over by FDIC.

- Go all in on equities as corporations begin to declare improving profits due to prior layoffs.

When inflation is declared dead and deflation becomes the major risk, paupers will typically sell their good investments at rock bottom prices. But be wary of buying excessive amounts of company bonds or stocks near bankruptcy.

These changes can be made over time and don't necessarily require a complete shift in all investments. Core investments can be held for decades with small percentage changes, allowing the balanced portfolio to respond to corresponding indicator changes. Some investments can adjust to these changes as they mature.

Always consult with the appropriate investment, tax and legal professionals before making portfolio changes. Potentially adverse unintended consequences can occur with every change.

Taxes aren't a problem in most retirement accounts but often cause problems for nonqualified or taxed-as-you-go investments. Later I will discuss how to choose an investment advisor.

The Annual Cycle

The random walk theory would have you believe that every day of the year investments have an equal likelihood of going up or down. Most investors have heard of the Sell In May And Go Away summer slump and the Year End Rally.

There are numerous other anomalies that can affect our less than random walk as investors. I will focus here on the tendency of lower-risk positive returns to occur from October through February.

Most institutional investors try to put their best foot forward when preparing annual statements. There's a tendency to make portfolio changes—called window dressing—three to six months before the end of the year, usually during the summer or early fall months.

Businesses often enjoy their best news of the year in January. Improved Christmas sales, new product introductions, optimistic sales projections and higher profits just before or after the end of the year are contributing factors.

Rumors of an improved business environment may begin to filter in around November. Businesses often report bad news while everyone is on vacation during the summer, hoping it will be ignored.

Election outcomes in the U. S. are most uncertain about three to six months prior to November. Virtually every recent election had times when either side experienced an uptick in popularity.

Remember, the stock market hates uncertainty. Regardless of which side wins, a group of stocks will benefit and another group will suffer.

There are numerous tax-related reasons why investors will sell or hold stocks. Small-cap stocks that lose money during the year tend to continue to sell off through December 31, allowing investors to lock in the tax losses. Those same stocks tend to be repurchased in January. That tendency to gain value is called the January Effect.

Lacking a season like Christmas to drive sales, stock reports tend to be less energetic and more uncertain during the summer months. Every other year there's an election in November that raises the uncertainty.

According to the Stock Trader's Almanac, since 1950, the Dow Jones Industrial Average has average returns only a fraction over 0.3 percent during the May-October period, compared with an average gain of 7.5 percent during the November-April period.

This pattern is interrupted or enhanced by recession years like 2008-2009 or could be even more pronounced depending on whether the boom bust market cycle begins or ends during summer or winter.

As a result of the deep selloffs from the recession of 2008-2009, the year-end rally didn't happen. The markets didn't recover until the summer of 2009, when they experienced robust gains.

Covid19 caused an unnaturally sharp recession beginning in March, 2020. This caused the natural usual summer slowdown to be absent. The wise investor should recognize and pay attention to the 4–8-year cycles as they will overwhelm the annual cycles.

The most dramatic selloff in stock market history happened on October 19, 1987, when the Dow Jones Industrial Average lost 508.2 points—over 22%—in one day! I have a copy of the Wall Street Journal on my wall to remind me of that spectacular buying opportunity.

September 11, 2001 somehow happened during the Investment Bermuda Triangle period of the year. The buying opportunity as a result didn't occur until two weeks later, since trading was halted after the tragedy.

If something is going to break down, it seems to happen between May and October. Stock market bubbles often burst during this period. Perhaps this time of year has developed a mystique based on the legendary crash of October 28, 1929.

The stock markets in the United States and the world seemed to have a normal appearing year-end rally in 2021. Black Swan events can occur anytime, like a war in Ukraine. Whenever the news is all negative, there's uncertainty or unusual events occur these cycles can be interrupted.

I am skeptical by nature and can imagine a conspiracy that manipulates the markets so that rich people can buy the good investments of gullible investors at rock-bottom prices.

There's no evidence of this; it's just the natural respiration of the stock market organism. If a conspiracy is someday uncovered, I would like to get credit for recognizing it early.

There are many lessons to learn from the patterns of prior years. Remember that every future year will play out in its own way. God granted mankind free will.

It seems paupers are determined to exercise their free will to sell their great quality investments at rock-bottom prices during the summer and early fall. Wise investors learn from this and will do the exact opposite of the pauper.

All portfolio changes should be considered for tax consequences, liquidity, market, interest rate and inflation risk, and personal temperament before trading on any of these patterns.

Occasionally, the markets have gone down as expected, befitting the summer slump, only to continue to go down after, as they did in the summer of 2008, not reaching a true low until March

9, 2009. Remember, recession years are tricky. Reread the boom recession cycle explanation earlier in this chapter.

This Sell in May and Go Away strategy accompanied by a Reinvest in Early Fall strategy helps achieve two positive portfolio results: Likely locking in profits from the prior Year End Rally and becoming more conservative.

This is also a somewhat aggressive investment strategy because it facilitates investing at a market bottom, should a summer or early fall sell off in stocks occur. If you are wrong about getting out of more-aggressive stocks in May, get back into the markets at the appropriate time in late summer or early fall before the year-end rally.

Taking Action

Here's a list of action items you should consider to take advantage of paupers that want to sell their good investments cheap during the summer.

1. In late spring, build an appropriate percentage of your portfolio into conservative liquid investments, such as high-quality, short-duration bonds and FDIC insured cash deposits. Most low-volatility, high-quality liquid investments will fit the bill.

2. Choose an appropriate time to "get conservative." It's not so much the date that determines when to trade as it is what the market is doing at the time. This will vary from year to year. When the market is up an attractive percentage of say 6 to 10% or more and on a roll in April or May, paupers tend to invest more, driving stock prices higher. Wise investors could harvest some stock market gains of 6% or more.

3. Be patient. If you decide against trading and the market experiences its summer slump, don't panic. Just be a buy and hold investor and ride it out. Buy and hold investors average between 9-11%[14]. It could take a few years to recover after a selloff, but you will be fine.

4. Although difficult to pinpoint, watch for signs of market capitulation—the moment when pauper investors give up on recovering their losses and sell their good stuff for whatever price they can get. There will be rampant selling and little demand for stock. The press will pile on the bad news. There might be days when the markets experience unrestrained volatility. Record high volume and volatility usually mark the highest opportunity days. Paupers are selling everything they own.

5. If you choose to move investments around, chances are you may get out—and get back in—on less than optimal days. But you are likely to have a lower risk than buy and hold investors. I often would like to be a little early to the trading party, therefore never getting the highest prices but getting close when selling and never getting the lowest prices when buying.

6. Dollar cost averaging (DCA) in and out of the markets removes the emotion and timing out of investment decisions. It involves selling a percentage of your aggressive stock or bond holdings each in April, May and June, slowly building your conservative positions. Try to trade on days during these months when the markets have been up.

7. The next DCA step is to slowly sell your conservative positions and begin to buy back aggressive positions. Trade in August, September, and October. As a rule, choose to buy more aggressive investments that are down the most. Balance the portfolio and avoid gambling behavior. Sell conservative investments and

buy aggressive investments on days when the markets are down. Capitulation doesn't happen every year but consider going all in if you recognize it.

This is NOT contrarian investing. This style of investing involves selling high and buying low. There's nothing contrarian about that. Paupers want you to buy their quality investments.

The institutional titans are fueling the fears of the paupers. During these moments, the system is ripe for you to feast on a buffet of affordable quality investments. Just get your game face on, open your eyes and recognize the opportunities presented. Carpe diem: Seize the day.

Final Thoughts on Predictions

Impressed by someone who claims to have a system for predicting the markets, paupers sink everything into an investment managed by some charismatic or hot fund manager— or worse, by some fraudulent con artist. They assume that having examined all the data, the manager can discern a pattern.

These "experts" are paid millions—and often billions in the case of hedge fund managers—precisely because they're supposed to be able to see the pattern. And yet these famous prognosticators frequently fail to do any better than chance.

According to a 2008 Performance Perspectives by iShares, after fees and taxes, the average actively managed fund outperformed its index only 23 percent of the time across all investment categories and time frames.

That means roughly 77 percent of all actively managed stock fund managers underperform their index. The few that do outperform their peers are drowned by more money than could be successfully invested using their strategies going forward. These funds typically evolve from nimble predators to lumbering wooly mammoths.

Style drift and size invariably take a toll on performance. Buying the hottest-performing investment makes sense only if it is an appropriately proportional part of a balanced portfolio.

Remember what we said previously about reverting to the mean? Funds over perform because they are unbalanced. That lack of balance can cause them to eventually become losers.

It's unlikely there are any true geniuses managing investment funds. The managers might be able to overcome some of the shortfalls of average investors, but they also have serious restrictions on their management practices.

Managers strive to have a high percentage of their fund always invested. Even if they believe the stock market is likely to fall, their prospectus requires the fund remain invested most of the time. Turnover inside the fund can also take a toll.

According to a Wall Street Journal article, total costs can run as high as 1.97% percent a year. In addition to an average administration and management fee of 1.31 percent a year, and the median trading cost could be .66 percent or higher.[15] From the article:

"The average investor can't really even begin to get a strong grasp on these additional costs," says Richard Kopcke, an economist at the Center for Retirement Research at Boston College who co- wrote a recent study about fees and trading costs of mutual funds in 401k plans. "There's just not enough information. Not even close."

Choosing a stock fund that has recently outperformed likely means picking an investment loaded with bank, tech, oil or precious metals stocks—just as those markets are starting to regress to the mean or even crash. Yet this is exactly what pauper investors and their advisors tend to do. Funds that outperform one year consistently receive the lion's share of investments the following year.

The financial media and fund family tout the highflying performer. Some advisors think they are helping their clients by presenting only the outperforming funds: "Nothing but Five Star funds for you, sir!"

Sadly, the current underperformers that are likely to be the overperformers next year never make it to the recommended list. The deck is stacked against investors, whether they pick their own stocks or employ an advisor.

Equity fund investors typically experience lower results than the funds bought and held. For the twenty-year period from 1987 through 2007, the average equity fund bought and held, without trading and with dividends reinvested, yielded 10.81 percent while the average equity fund investor gained only 4.48 percent.[16]

So let's once again give the hottest new investment the Duck Test. What does an over-hyped investment look like?

- It gets five stars from the rating agencies.

- The fund manager is featured in the Wall Street Journal.

- Money Magazine names it a "Best Fund" for the next decade.

- The manager writes a book about stock picking strategy.

- The investment has a great track record that is already starting to recede by the time you hear about it.

If you are picking a stock or fund for the long term, you might want to avoid the hottest issues. Funds sometimes outperform in the short term by taking high risks, concentrating the portfolio into a narrow sector, or merely by blind luck.

These funds invariably experience lower-than-average returns as they revert back to the mean. The star managers of these funds are also likely to move on to greener pastures.

In closing this chapter, I want to warn you about trying to predict what will happen by reading or listening to the news. Most news is counterintuitive.

You, your advisor and everyone on the evening news might think something is negative, while the stock market sees it as a positive. Here's a short list of news items that can easily be misinterpreted:

1. High unemployment could be interpreted by the stock market as increased productivity, and the FED is likely to stimulate the economy. That's usually good for stocks.

2. Rising interest rates often are interpreted as a negative for investments, but the money must go somewhere. While high-quality bonds with long durations are likely to lose value during rising interest rate environments, stock values may increase.

3. Record government debt could be interpreted as foretelling rising inflation, but when will that inflation hit? Knowing when something is going to happen can be more important than knowing it will happen.

4. Record low approval ratings for the President or Congress can be interpreted by the stock market as there's likely to be a change in Washington come the next election cycle.

5. The negatives are cooked into the pie. Future predictions of negative events can be overblown. The positives aren't known or revealed yet. Sometimes a stock market bottom is revealed when very bad news happens and the stock market goes up. Be patient.

It sounds counterintuitive, but bad news can often be interpreted as good news for investments. When you are having an especially difficult day and your body is oozing with every stress hormone known to man or woman, please, please, please don't sell your good investments. Remember our APT steps from the Introduction: Acknowledge you are having a bad day with a lot of stressors; Pause and take a breather; Think how you may be misinterpreting the bad news. This is likely to be just the break your weary brain needs to get control.

Chapter Four

The Herd Mentality

*Men, it has been well said, think in herds; it
will be seen that they go mad in herds,
while they only recover their senses slowly,
and one by one.*
Charles Mackay

Let's return once more to prehistory, where lions, bears and wolves were the most successful predators on earth. Responding to this threat, a single shout from a troop mate would spur every one of your ancestors into coordinated action. The troop might freeze in place, hoping that a dangerous predator wouldn't see them, run for cover by climbing a tree, or rally a furious counterattack using sticks and stones. That group unity must have worked pretty well; otherwise, the troop would have died in an attack, and you would not be here.

Modern man retains the same three responses to distress signals when it comes to investing, often mounting a simultaneous collective response. This social coordination explains the massive rises and crashes in stock markets. The mass media, internet, and now social media can exacerbate the impact by spreading information worldwide almost instantaneously.

Dorothy Cheney, Robert Seyfarth[17], and their assistants did extensive research into primate alarm calls in baboon, vervet monkeys, and other species. Vervet monkeys have distinct danger calls to warn the troop about eagles or snakes. We can conclude that humans have been giving and receiving alarm calls for tens of millions of years. Today, investors are predisposed to hearing, reacting, and overreacting to the alarm calls of stock analysts, financial writers and newscasters. We react much like our primate relatives, albeit with some 21st century twists.

Vervet Monkey

No wonder the stock market experienced record volatility in 2008. The VIX index, a measure of volatility of the S&P 500 Index, soared to record highs twice during October and November of 2008.[18] Let's take a moment to contemplate how our not-so-modern responses present themselves during such volatile times.

Freeze

When investors sniff danger, they may freeze and be unwilling to make corrective decisions. Uncertainty clouds their thinking:

"Maybe the danger will abate or pass by. We can't really be in recession, can we?"

If the markets have been performing well recently and the collective outlook is positive, it can be difficult for investors to envision a significant downturn.

Cheney and Seyfarth's vervet monkeys had this reaction when one in the troop detected a snake. A warning call is shouted out; troop members freeze and look around until the snake is located. Then, working as a team to reduce the danger, another call goes out, and the troop retreats to safety.

The freeze response can be an effective strategy, assuming investors have the discipline to stick with it and leave everything alone through a whole cycle. Savvy investors want better information before they act on the initial warning call. In reality, there are so many warning calls being shouted out that it's difficult to determine which are genuine threats that need to be acted upon. Investors are constantly besieged with calls to abandon their balanced portfolio strategy and shift everything into a defensive asset. Investors who can ignore the noise and maintain a buy and hold strategy with a balanced portfolio could be the most successful over the long term.

Just as vervet monkeys scan their environment when threatened, investors should seek additional information when confronted with a freeze alarm call. When threatened, it only makes sense to try to learn all we can about the threat. While the monkeys can quickly detect whether or not a snake is nearby, investors do not always have that luxury when it comes to gleaning information about a stock. I suspect every press release issued by Enron contained false information, right up until the firm collapsed.

You should consider the freeze strategy (buy and hold) as an alternative to potentially overreacting to the shouts of danger. If you freeze early in an economic downturn, resolve to stay with your buy and hold strategy throughout the entire cycle. The following graphic illustrates the four stages in a major cycle of stocks, stock sectors, or the stock market as a whole:

- Consolidation or base building phase: Often called the accumulation phase. Institutional buyers are accumulating shares on the dips.

- Upward advancement phase: Called the markup phase or rapid growth phase in the stock business. Institutional buyers are holding positions they acquired during the consolidation/base building phase. Smaller astute investors are buying the stock.

- Culmination or distribution phase: When most professionals take profits selling on the rips. The public continues to buy. Paupers notice a hot stock and are buying...usually near the top.

- Decline or markdown phase: Anyone still holding the position is losing money. Paupers continue to buy on the way down until near the bottom, when they often sell in a panic.

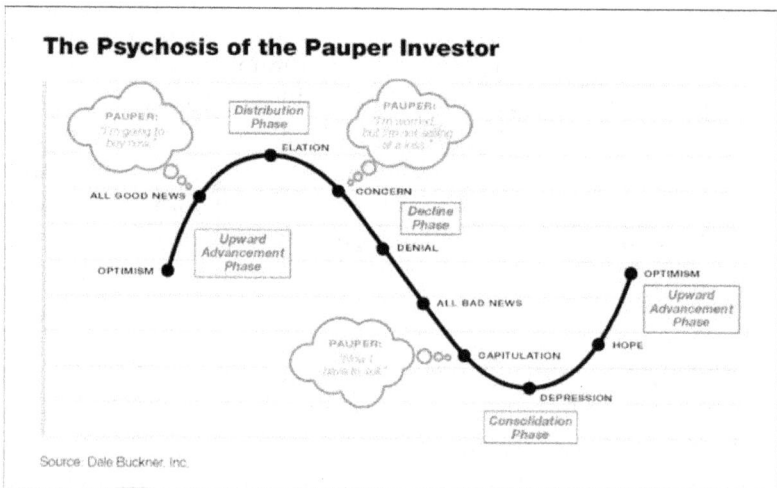

The Psychosis of the Pauper Investor

Source: Dale Buckner, Inc.

If a quality stock reaches the decline phase and you own it, simply wait until the stock starts at the first stage again. When it's upward advancement increases, you can sell. Warren Buffet, arguably the most successful stock investor ever, advises buying good companies and holding them...sometimes forever.

Of course, freezing, then panicking at the bottom is the worst strategy you can choose. This ensures you will sell close to the most recent bottom, virtually guaranteeing you have locked in a permanent loss.

Run for Cover

When the stock market suffers a significant drop, many investors want to sell everything quickly to get to "safe ground," just as if they were running for the nearest tree to escape a snake. In their panic, they believe selling is the safest alternative. Their thinking is "If I sell now, at least my investments won't be worthless."

If huge numbers of investors combine the run for cover reaction with herding behavior, the stock market can experience a dramatic drop, as it did October 19, 1987, when the DJIA lost 22.6 percent, its worst one-day decline in history. I have that copy of the October 20, 1987, Wall Street Journal to remind me of the spectacular buying opportunity that morning.

Modern man has added 24/7 news and computer technology to the information mix. Throw in computerized trading, and the market is vulnerable to a one-day decline like we witnessed on May 6th, 2010 —called the "flash crash"[19]—when a trading error and investor panic caused a near-collapse of the stock market.

The stock exchange operator NASDAQ OMX Group canceled thousands of trades after numerous stocks plunged to a fraction of their normal values.

Social Media and fractionalized, biased news reporting have also increased in recent years. Most news appears to have a political agenda that results in the listener hating the "other" side.

Conservatives hate liberals and liberals hate conservatives. Baby boomers hate millennials, millennials hate baby boomers. You tell me who you are and I'll tell you the blogger that wants you to hate another group. This adds fuel to the emotional fires and makes the volatility of the stock market even more pronounced.

What happens when everyone sells at the same time? Predictably, the market for securities dries up. Stocks plummet below their intrinsic and book values because there's no one willing to purchase them. Share prices might fall far below what analysts would have thought possible.

Investors selling at such a moment might experience a loss of principal that could last a lifetime. There are anecdotal stories of investors who sold out during October 1987, and never bought stocks again.

John Maynard Keynes called these deviations from classic economic theory animal spirits.[20] Depressions are caused by pervasive irrational pessimism. The stock market crash of 1929 did NOT cause the depression. A combination of irrational pessimism and government policies altered the collective perception from the optimism of the 1920s to the pessimism of the 1930s.

The mob rule of the 1930s kept the money supply tight and the consumer from spending. The government raised taxes and trade barriers; people demanded it. Capitalistic enterprises suffered, and government became an increasingly larger employer in America.

When people are free to do as they please,
they usually imitate each other.
Eric Hoffer

The 21st century investor may have an overwhelming compulsion to join the mob. When everyone else appears to be jumping off the cliff, the idea no longer seems absurd. Some investors describe the experience thusly: "I would rather sell now while everyone else is selling, even if I might be wrong, than wait and experience any more loss on my own."

If you can recognize the mob direction and do the opposite, you can reap better, safer investment results. Develop skills to interpret the "alarm calls" of other investors.

You should Think Rich and Make Money! It should not be viewed as counterintuitive to stop, pause, and keep your good stocks and bonds, or to buy low and sell high or buy stock while all around you are selling.

Counterattack!

Look at market fluctuations as your friend rather than your enemy; profit from folly rather than participate in it.
Warren Buffet

The third vervet monkey reaction against a predator is to send out the call to mount a counterattack against the perceived threat. Investors can do the same thing by buying when the news is bad.

Interpreting the warnings correctly could allow you to determine if this is an opportunity to invest with lower prices and less risk or if the warnings represent real threat. This strategy might backfire on an investor with individual stocks but has a high chance for success when investing in the broader indices.

If you are ever going to buy low, it will likely be a time when there is pervasive bad news. I repeat: bad news means good stock prices; good news means bad stock prices. Isn't that messed up?

The stock markets will predict the direction of the news six to twelve months in advance. Many investors closely follow unemployment reports, but unemployment reports are considered trailing indicators.

An astute investor should be invested before there is an improvement in the employment numbers. If you wait until employment has significantly improved, you are likely to have missed a good percentage of the gains during a cycle.

Our ancient ancestors would pick up sticks and stones and attack a threatening predator. Modern day investors respond with anger. Lawyers are hired. Articles are written and now social media lights up, blaming whomever is in charge in Washington, DC.

It was appalling but perhaps not surprising to witness the anger directed at AIG employees and their families after Congress and the SEC gave billions of dollars of 2008 TARP money to the firm to prevent it from declaring bankruptcy. Protestors argued that it wasn't fair AIG executives received millions in bonuses paid for by Uncle Sam.

British Petroleum got a dose of anger reaction over the Deepwater Horizon oil spill. Investors couldn't pick up sticks and rocks to throw at BP, but they could sue and did. There have been a record number of lawsuits against investment companies, financial analysts, and corporations. I'm not sure if the injured investors ever get much out of these lawsuits but at least they feel better.

The National Debt has ballooned almost out of control with all the Covid19 relief funds that were handed out by both political parties. Emotions can run high during times like this.

For the most part, the stock market doesn't care. If a company sells more $4.00 tubes of toothpaste, more $5.00 hamburgers or more expensive cars, its stock goes up. It doesn't matter who is in control in Washington. I warn most investors not to confuse anger about the news cycle with sound investment strategy.

As wise investors, it is our jobs to be less political and more opportunistic. Like the sailing ship, determine where you want to go and plot your course. Determine how the wind is blowing. Tack the sails accordingly. Monitor your course constantly with minor adjustments. Make sure you are in open water. Monitor the weather.

As investors we shouldn't care how the political winds are blowing. With appropriate attention, you can get to your goal of a safe, growing income and principal your entire life, no matter which party or politician is in office.

Gullibility

Our instincts entice us to buy overpriced investments. We buy because our friends, media "experts" or slick marketing campaigns convince us to buy.

Here's an example of modern behavior that could yield disastrous results. In the fall of 2010, gold prices were near record levels after the deep panic and stock market selloff of 2008-2009. Advertisements with trusted celebrities touting gold coins as the only safe investment seemed to be on every radio and television commercial break.

There weren't enough gold coins to meet the temporary demand, so some gold coins were selling for far more than their bullion value. All this was good news for investors, who bought gold early in the rally and then sold. On the other hand, for investors about to buy gold, it was a potential disaster.

Gold bullion appreciated to a high of over $1,800 an ounce[21] in September 2011. Gold didn't return to these lofty prices until 2022, when on July 28, 2021 spot gold prices were $1,806 an ounce at the close of trading according to Yahoo! Finance.

At this point, there was a supply and demand problem for gold coins that temporarily drove "collectible" gold coin prices up. This can continue if the economy lags or inflation is deemed to be a problem in the future. The demand for gold coins can only continue to rise if the world experiences an even deeper recession, hyperinflation or a calamitous event like a worldwide natural disaster or major international war.

The SEC in 2021 had a cease-and-desist order against a large gold bullion marketing firm that convinced senior investors to sell their stock funds and other security holdings. The fear pitch was that the solid stock investments could become worthless during the next market crash. The firm was charging a 25% commission that was undisclosed.

Should the economy level off or begin to improve, gold investors might want to sell to get cash to invest into stocks or other investments. Remember, gold coins do not pay dividends, nor do they split from growth, as do some stocks.

Another consideration is that, at the top of the market, gold coins could be priced as high as twice the market value of the gold they contain. If spot gold is selling for $2,000 an ounce, a temporarily rare gold coin containing ½ ounce of spot gold worth $1,000 could sell for $2,000.

Should demand for gold subside due to an economic upswing, the price of gold could drop to $1,000 a spot ounce, and that ½ ounce gold coin could drop to spot-ounce prices.

Suddenly, that coin is no longer rare or in demand. Should that type of plunge occur, investors who purchased gold coins at $2,000 in March 2009, might be saddled with selling out for the gold spot price of $500, losing 75 percent of their original investment. This has also happened to silver coins in the past.

By the way, in July 2014, gold had retreated from its September, 2011, high of over $1,800 to a little over $1,300 an ounce, a drop of approximately 28 percent.

Gold briefly reached an all-time intraday high of $2,085 in March, 2022 due to uncertainty over the Ukraine/Russia War. The highest gold prices have happened during gut-churning uncertainty.

The reports that gold is the only safe investment or the only investment that's always made money are false advertising. Gold is a collectible and not a security. Gold vendors aren't held to the same fiduciary or best interest standards and advertising standards as securities, stocks and bonds.

Who made money in all this? Certainly, the media profited from the advertising revenue. The marketers of gold coins made money from the significant markup and profit margin. Rarely do investors make money on gold coins, because they are illiquid and can't sell them at retail.

Gold held as a security is liquid and readily bought and sold by investors with very little cost. The friction caused by holding gold coins is eliminated. The investor gets the market price. If you buy low and sell high you make money.

As the world economy returns to health, collectible gold investors could lose their shirts. Like many other investors, gold bugs are extremely reluctant to admit a mistake and could be stuck with their coins until the next gold coin cycle, possibly decades from now. We will discuss Confirmation Bias in a future chapter about Behavioral Finance.

Typically, the next "angry" step in a boom-and-bust cycle is the lawsuits filed by disgruntled investors against the collectible gold coin marketers. If you wish to have a bit of fun, Google "gold coin lawsuit" and see how many hits you get.

While reading this book, you should consider whether cyclical investments are closer to their peak or closer to the bottom. Every investment that goes up can also come down, sometimes even more rapidly than it ascended.

There are more destructive behaviors that can derail a successful investment strategy. Hoarding is often associated with gold investing from the beginning of time. The ancient story of Midas was likely written about a real person who lost everything because he coveted gold.

It is health that is real wealth and not pieces of gold and silver.
Mahatma Gandhi

Many gold investors also exhibit denial of loss, another form of bias. A recent advertisement said that "stocks can lose their value but gold is never worthless." Gold doesn't pay a dividend, doesn't grow in sales, make a profit, have industrial uses or have a stock split. Think about that the next time you have an urge to buy gold.

Tulip Mania and Other Folly

History has produced some truly spectacular and glaring instances where a mania took hold and produced disastrous results. One famous instance occurred in Holland in the 1630's.

A description of this mania is contained in the great economic treatise, Extraordinary Popular Delusions and the Madness of Crowds, written by British journalist Charles Mackay. He explains how tulips were a popular status symbol in the late 16th century in the Netherlands.

A particularly attractive variety owed its multiple colors to a "tulip-breaking virus". Because of the virus, these tulips weren't very hardy. Normal tulip reproduction from seed or asexual bulblet clones would take three to seven years before blooming.

This helped stimulate a futures market for the bulbs, which were selling for as much as 10 times the annual salary of a skilled craftsman.

The tulip bubble finally collapsed in March 1637. If you were among the last to own a bulb or bulb future, you lost everything. Up until that last month, there was always a buyer offering more money for your absurdly expensive bulbs.

There are numerous other examples of more recent bubbles and manias, such as the tech bubble of the late 1990s. It's hard to get a perspective on such an event when you are an active participant. Being able to recognize what a bubble looks like is critical. Paupers participate in bubbles without recognizing the danger.

Most bubbles are preceded by a rapid uptick in the price of the investment near the end of the bubble. The most astute investors will recognize there's a bubble and will short the investment or sell borrowed stock. This strategy is very risky.

If the market continues to go higher, they will want to get back in to reduce loses. They must buy the investment back at ever-higher prices, thus feeding the bubble even more. This is called "covering your shorts," due to a short squeeze. Paupers commonly buy into the tail end of bubbles.

But speculative bubbles aren't the most damaging herd behavior. There's often an equally robust herding reaction during every recession or depression. Selling quality investments at the bottom of a selloff can make you poor forever.

Let's do the Duck Test again just to see what a bubble and other herding behavior looks like so that you can avoid it.

- Prices of the stock or investment have never been as high.

- People are apt to borrow money, go on margin, to buy more of the investment.

- The hype is persuasive. In the case of the tech bubble, the argument was that the economy had changed forever.

- The most unsophisticated people are buying into the bubble. Investors with very small amounts of money and who had never invested were scooping up shares of Cisco near the end of the tech bubble.

- The entire investment community seems to be wildly optimistic or pessimistic.

- The bubble receives nonstop media coverage. Every other advertisement seems to be pitching the investment.

- Fundamental investment analysis says that the intrinsic value of the investment is completely out of kilter with the current price—either high or low. In the case of tech stocks, there weren't any earnings to check.

- Investors exhibit gambling behavior.

- Investors exhibit panic behavior, such as fight or flight reactions.

If you have any question that you are reacting emotionally when investing, you should activate the APT decision-making system. Many investing errors could be avoided by simply pausing and thinking before acting.

The Securities and Exchange Commission (SEC) has issued several warnings about cryptocurrency, oil drilling and gold mining marketers and the deceptive and illegal practices they employ. The gambling behavior of some investors can be financially damaging.

Be warned that con artists are selling worthless cryptocurrency accounts, oil drilling programs and gold mining stocks. The pitch is instant wealth. There's often a bubble-like behavior exhibited by victims of a pump and dump scheme.

A pump and dump scam takes place when near worthless stock owned by a con artist is promoted to increase in value in the very near future. The value is pumped up by false claims like "ABC Pharmaceuticals has discovered the cure for all cancer." The claims are endless and are used to convince the next victim to buy at increasingly higher prices.

The con artist is selling the worthless stock at increasingly higher prices. The second phase happens when the ever-increasing glowing claims by the seller are stopped. The scammed are left with worthless stock that slowly goes to zero value as the con artist books their trip to a country without extradition agreements.

Tribal Loyalty

Many animal studies shed light on how ancient man was able to recognize troop mates almost instantly. They were programmed to feel more comfortable among their troop mates and family. Further, they felt safer when surrounded by familiar locations and landmarks.

To run an effective political party you need a degree of tribalism, it's the glue that holds everyone together.
Charles Kennedy

Modern man has, for lack of better word, a prejudice for the familiar. This prejudgment often creates the mistaken view that the company where we work is safer than other companies.

No knowledgeable investment advisor would advise investors to put all their nest egg into a single stock, but that is exactly what many a 401k, ESOP or Employee Stock Option Plan participant does. Advisors who condone such an investment strategy could be sued for malpractice if the stock should lose money due to a companywide collapse.

I wonder how many retirement dreams were ruined because of investments in Enron ESOPs or GM stock in 401ks as we witnessed GM turning into Government Motors. Strong companies can run into a series of bad management errors.

This strategy is doubly damaging when retirement nest eggs are invested into a company AND participants lose their jobs. An analogy is summarized by a quote from an investor who lost everything at ENRON: "It's like my best friend betrayed me."

Most financial advisors recommend no more than 10% to 20% in the stock of a company or industry where the client works. Even the strongest and largest companies can experience an Exxon Valdez or British Petroleum Deepwater Horizon event. Enron did it by falsifying their books. Many companies get into trouble by borrowing too much to expand too quickly.

Chapter Five

Man's View of the Future

*By far the greatest danger of Artificial
Intelligence is that people conclude too early
that they understand it.*
Eliezer Yudkowsky

The minute they began to harness technology, our ancient ancestors gained a distinct advantage over the less-intelligent creatures inhabiting their world. For them, technology meant being able to kill something with a rock or stick instead of their bare hands.

Our ancestors gained another advantage when fire was harnessed, allowing them to process vegetables, grains and animals that formerly caused diseases or were inedible.

Fire was believed to be discovered around 790,000 years ago in Israel and the popular press speculates that could have been as early as 1,400,000 years ago in Kenya. This technology stuff has been burning (pun intended) in us ever sense.

And once the spear was invented, the probability of success on a hunt increased tenfold. Once arrows were introduced, it was another leap for humans but both inventions are relatively recent introductions.

Our ancestors used stone tools to butcher animals even further back in time. In Bouri, Ethiopia bones with cut marks have been discovered that date back to 2.5 to 2.6 million years ago.

This technology explosion has helped our ancestors survive and thrive from the beginning. These inventions predate the introduction of modern humans.

These were early indications we were going to be a successful species. Man wasn't going to out-reproduce rival species, so we had to out-survive them. Survival wasn't assured until our ancestors accumulated a few other things that distinguished them from animals.

Language and communication certainly were important and don't forget about standing upright and the opposable thumb. I don't think of these things as technology, per se, but somewhere around 10,000 to 20,000 years ago, Homo sapiens developed technology to take advantage of their God- given body parts.

Technology isn't a new phenomenon. There have been numerous milestones since man first started tinkering with things. Agriculture, domesticating animals, the wheel and fishing helped our ancestors jumpstart another round of out-surviving their not-so-intelligent kin.

In more recent times, industrialization, electricity, the assembly line and the computer chip further advanced the transformation. Now artificial intelligence, space travel and better global commerce continue the survival march.

Recent DNA testing indicates that Neanderthals and Denisovans interbred with modern man.[22] But they didn't have a chance of outliving our ancestors, who were smarter and had better technology. Modern man had better civilization, technology, agriculture and genes.

Moore's Law – The number of transistors and resistors on a chip doubles every 24 months
Gordon Moore

Today, technology typically doubles every couple of years[23] and it isn't slowing down. Over five billion people in the world own a mobile device. Over 2.65 billion people use social media. Over 3.8 billion people have access to the internet.

Apple introduced its first iPhone on June 29, 2007. Every year or so, an updated version is introduced. I'm just guessing but I think that technology was pretty good for Apple stock.

Technology was also good for the thousands of companies that manufacture iPhone parts, assemble, sell, service and blog about iPhones, and the corner Starbucks near the Apple store.

Technology like the iPhone has transformed the developing world. China has a whole city built around assembling the iPhone and the country has transformed into a manufacturing powerhouse during the past decades.

If you believe the Chinese government's figure, the country's economy as measured by GNP is growing at 6.6 to 10 percent a year. The education and training they've received will likely benefit the individual workers for the remainder of their lives, long after the iPhone ceases to exist.

Technology rarely retreats. The technology that ultimately replaces the iPhone will be equally amazing. Productivity increases. Prices go down. Jobs are destroyed and created.

Man has enjoyed an increasingly higher standard of living from the moment our ancestors harnessed fire and built the first tools. This isn't going to change. Technology marches forward.

I conclude that technology was the driving force that allowed Homo sapiens to survive, succeed and out-compete all other species on earth. Every stock in a balanced portfolio benefits from technology improvements. Technology improvements are going to continue. Buy stocks and get the growth.

The Cave

Every person who invests in well selected real estate in a growing section of a prosperous community adopts the surest and safest method of becoming independent, for real estate is the basis of wealth.
Theodore Roosevelt

Our ancestors sought prime real estate with the same advantages we value today: a good location, stable roof, protection from the elements and external threats, and convenient access to food and clothing. Several cave systems have had hominid inhabitance for 2 to 3 million years. The real estate market has been flourishing ever since.

Technology has allowed mankind to expand into every niche of the globe. I even had a relative who lived at the South Pole! It's my contention that ever since man learned how to own and sell real estate, it's been appreciating at about three percent a year. If there are oil resources or minerals under the land, multiply that number by one hundred.

One of mankind's best inventions was ownership. Until relatively recently, people would simply steal the land from whoever was perceived to be too weak to defend it. While the ancient world developed rudimentary ownership laws, they were expanded and perfected in England, making it possible to buy and sell property efficiently and at relatively low cost. Today, almost anyone can profit from purchasing real estate and the potential riches that might lie under it.

Property rights and the freedom to own real estate are improving in most nations. That's good news for the creation of wealth and for investing worldwide.

According to a Zippia.com report dated April 5, 2022,[24] there are an estimated 22,000,000 millionaires in America. That means that 8.8% of US adults are millionaires. 33% of those millionaires are women.

There are also an estimated 9,000,000 millionaire households in China, Japan, Taiwan, and Hong Kong. China alone has over 5,000,000 millionaires. That there are now millionaires living in nations spread across the globe contributes to world peace and stability.

Germany is unlikely to attack its neighbors for fear of losing its trading partners. China is unlikely to launch an economic attack on America because it would devastate its own economy. There's simply too much at risk, and all this helps solidify the safety and stability of your investments. Don't underestimate the probability that stocks and real property worldwide will appreciate.

The Russian war against Ukraine is likely to be an exception. Russian millionaires don't even come up on the top ten nations list. According to Trading Economics, the 2021 GDP of the Russian Federation is $1.775 Trillion, which represents only 1.33% of world GDP. When it comes down to it, Russia has become a nuclear power that's economically poor, making them dangerous.

Society and Civilization

Another great invention was civilization. For tens of thousands of years, our ancestors wandered around as nomads or squatters. They plundered and murdered anyone different from them and took anything they wanted if they thought they could get away with it.

Knowing some Viking[25] was likely to bash your head in and take everything you owned discouraged wealth development and property ownership. Please don't be insulted. I have Viking blood in my veins, though all my family can be traced back to England, Scotland, Wales, and Ireland.

Civilization is likely to continue to reduce wars that disrupt and damage wealth creation. However, wars are not always bad for investments. As previously mentioned, war can be good for some stocks because in the modern age it is often concluded in weeks.

War stimulates industry and technology. People buy weapons. People break things that must be fixed. War tends to settle disagreements between nations more quickly now.

Don't get me wrong, I am not advocating war. I advocate free trade. And given everyone is in everyone else's pocket, modern nations are less likely to attack each other. Free trade has been gaining steam to the benefit of peace and prosperity worldwide.

Free trade has transformed the nations that embraced it. The emerging markets[26] are ripe with entrepreneurial spirit. It's hard to pick a winner as there are so many that are outperforming.

In 2010, I conducted a study of unemployment rates and found that while America topped 10 percent, China was around 4 percent, and Peru, of all places, was about 7 percent.

Where there is job creation, there's profit. There are so many more jobs being created in the emerging world than in the developed world. I believe emerging markets should be part of virtually any balanced investment portfolio.

America retains the world's largest manufacturing base, followed by China. America hasn't reduced manufacturing; China has been growing it. This is likely to be good for investments worldwide.

Emerging markets represent huge opportunities to grow markets for U.S. goods. Kentucky Fried Chicken, Starbucks, The

Gap, and American toothpaste are finding a market around the world because of prosperity and free trade.

According to Forbes.com, the top brand names in the world are Apple, Google, Microsoft, Amazon, Facebook, Coca-Cola and Disney. American brand names dominate the world with 32 of the top 50 brand names.

America is conquering the world one latte at a time. Or is China conquering the world by being prosperous and buying our latte? I see the free flow of ideas and technology to be the future cement that binds mankind together. Friendly competition is healthy for countries as well as business. That's good for investments, too.

The developing countries[27] stand to benefit the most from computer technology. My sister-in-law gets up every morning, turns on her computer, checks her email and checking account, and pays her bills with a credit card. She works from home. She signs on to Facebook, Skypes with loved ones and has a relatively normal day that might happen anywhere in America.

The fact that she lives on a remote island in the middle of the South Pacific Ocean nation of Fiji is more remarkable. Many of the benefits of the computer age have made it to Fiji and every other corner of the world.

The benefits of technology are transforming the world, and the best is yet to come. The adventure didn't stop with the invention of fire; it was just getting started. I am optimistic regarding the future. I suggest you adopt the same perspective.

The discussion now isn't whether computers are learning; it's how a machine is deep learning and whether a machine can have feelings. I'm fortunate to have access to advanced information on the subject. I'm hoping those apocalyptic stories like "The Terminator" or the novel "1984" will never come true.

I Googled "How scary is the Google algorithm." On June 14, 2022, Google employee Blake Lemoine was put on paid leave after claiming that Lamda AI, an artificial intelligence chatbot, had become sentient. Lemoine asserts that his machine friend was displaying the behavior of a seven to eight-year-old child.

Professor Melanie Mitcher at the Santa Fe Institute studies and teaches AI. She claims that humans project human feelings onto the words generated by computer code in a process called anthropomorphism. My editor just said no one will read another word after that one, but the tech ride will be something to see during your lifetime.

The Dark Side of Mankind

I have listened to a chorus of negative news my entire career. "The best days are behind us; the United States is heading for collapse; Social Security is bankrupt; the national debt is too high; the dollar will be worthless; the world economy is a house of cards; investors lose half of their wealth during economic downturns; the only thing that will be safe is...(insert whatever the pitch man is selling here)."

Don't be misled by hyperbole. Never let the fear mongers convince you to tie your money up in a poorly designed investment product with high costs and a multi-decade penalty to get your money back.

Fear tactics work so well that every market is rife with negative messages and sales pitches. Stand firm and stay positive. We have a tailwind behind us that is likely to propel balanced portfolios upward.

This is where the con artist invades the brains of paupers. They promise a guaranteed return, a guarantee of principal, and a "trust me" smile that wins over doubters. If you are offered an "investment opportunity" based on fear or greed, ask these questions:

1. What is the investment return dependent upon? Is it being paid from new inflows of money or from return on your original investment?

2. Is a properly trained and licensed professional handling the transaction? Securities-licensed professionals are held to a higher standard than those with only insurance licenses.

3. Does the person offering the investment have a CFP® professional designation, CERTIFIED FINANCIAL PLANNER™ Practitioner, RIA, Registered Investment Advisor, or AIF® Accredited Investment Fiduciary designation?

4. How long must you stay invested? What happens if you want to withdraw funds? What penalties, restrictions and procedures exist?

5. Can you readily monitor performance? What information do investment reports and updates contain and how often are they issued? Can you get reports and balances online easily?

6. Will your assets be held by a properly bonded and insured custodian, brokerage house, or bank? What are their credentials? Will anyone else have access to your account?

7. Is your account liquid? Can you cash out without administrative or exit penalties, contingent deferred sales charges (CDSC) or commissions? Were you appropriately informed about such fees? Did you sign a disclosure regarding the fees?

8. Did you check for complaints with the appropriate regulatory agency, such as your State Board of Insurance, State Securities Board, Better Business Bureau, or Real Estate Board?

9. Did you discuss the investment's internal fees? There are often administrative fees, riders, 12b1 fees, internal acquisition fees, marketing fees and rate caps that reduce your results. For example, some investment products cap stock market gains at one or two percent a month but allow unlimited downside capture.

10. What is the commission if applicable? A 10 percent commission doesn't materialize from thin air; it reduces your surrender value. Never accept the explanation, "You don't pay me anything; the insurance company pays me."

11. Is there a guarantee of principal or income? How much does that guarantee cost you? Is there more than an insurance company's promise backing up the guarantee? Is the guarantee simply a return of your own money?

The Long View

If you believe in the growth of technology, growth of real estate values and growth of stocks of solid companies. your investment approach should reflect that confidence. You have a supporting tailwind. Companies, countries and society in general are likely to do better in the future.

If you bet against technology, stocks and real estate, you are likely to lose. The economy is destined to improve. And when things appear darkest, it should be a signal to load up on brand-name investments that paupers are willing to sell cheap. Buy with both hands.

If you sell in response to bad news, you will likely be reacting with your pauper brain. Record stock market volume and dramatically lower prices often coincide with bad news. If you take anything from this book, it should be this:

Record low stockholder sentiment is one of the best indicators of a pending stock market bottom.
Dale Buckner

Here are some buying opportunities that may sound like horrible news but could be the perfect time to load up:

- War or military conflict is often good for stock prices, which are likely to experience a correction before conflict is declared.

- Stocks are apt to drop in price during economic turmoil or recession, which makes it a good time to buy.

- Stock prices tend to react positively to dropping long-term interest rates. Short-term rate increases have a negative effect on stocks. An inverted yield curve, where long-term interest rates are below short-term interest rates, is extremely negative for future stock prices. Sell in anticipation of much better opportunities to come.

- Political turmoil, such as an assassination or impeachment, will likely drive stock prices lower, creating a buying opportunity. Political turmoil in a company can lower its price. Once the CEO is replaced the stock already will be on the rise.

- High unemployment depresses shareholder sentiment, creating an environment to accumulate stocks. The Federal Reserve Board often stimulates the economy when this occurs. Conversely, low unemployment might signal the FED will tighten because of inflationary pressures. This would be a time to lighten up on stocks and consider safe haven investments like long treasury bonds or utilities.

- When the FED lowers short-term interest rates, lower bond holdings and accumulate stocks; when the FED raises short-term interest rates, reduce stock holdings and consider long quality bond investments

- If the mass media predicts the economy might be in imminent collapse (as they did on October 26, 2008,) it could be an ideal time to buy stocks.

- When investor sentiment is negative, it's likely a good time to sell gold investments. When investor concerns are low, it's more likely to be a good time to buy gold.

If we agree that paying lower prices for something is better, bad news is good news when it comes to buying most stocks. Conversely, hyped good news is good news when you wish to sell stocks. The pauper brain will invariably seize the inappropriate action.

There will usually be more than one right answer to a dilemma. Always consider the tax implications. There are times when lower-risk investments or conversion to cash might be in your best interests. Evaluate the alternatives without fear or greed and choose the most appropriate. When there is more than one right answer, diversify.

I recommend you become a conservative investor when others are buying higher-risk investments or lower quality.

Likewise, become a more aggressive investor when others are eager to sell their low-risk investments at rock-bottom prices. If the pauper side of your brain resists, hire a fiduciary advisor and follow his or her advice. What a concept: Hire professionals and take their advice.

I wish we lived in a world where the only governments were enlightened democracies. But we don't. There are things governments can do to enhance the benefits of mankind's progress.

Freedom, stable governments and equitable rules go a long way toward helping investors take advantage of the tailwind built into the economies of the world.

A Utopian wish list might include low-cost education, healthcare and energy for all, honest government, and at least minimal services for the developing world: clean water, immunizations, food, shelter, and freedom from terror and slavery and bigotry.

The Ukraine-Russian War dominated every headline. We are talking about approximately 2% of the world economy. The United States Federal Reserve Bank raising or lowering interest rates will affect the world economy much more. Rising short-term interest rates will tend to slow down 20% of the world economy directly and 50% indirectly.

It's important to know which news to ignore. It might take practice. I find that listening to economically unimportant news damages my reasoning. Bombings, terror attacks and mass shootings are often economically unimportant. Seeing the exceptionally historic event like 9/11 is obvious after the fact.

I'm seeing more significant economic news coming out about women's rights, race and gender discrimination and distrust of institutions. I'm even seeing a tendency to vilify our energy sources. I'd monitor these closely in the future.

Economies that allow women, minorities and gays to advance both politically and economically will do better than those that repress over half the population. Corrupt governments have existed from the beginning of civilization. Dictatorships have committed unspeakable atrocities from the beginning of time.

During Feudal Times, the world consisted of the nobility and the vassals and serfs. During Colonial Times, the world consisted of the oppressors and the oppressed. The rich and the poor gap hasn't improved much in modern times. What changed is that vast technology is available to virtually everyone. I'm optimistic.

I recommend you avoid investing in repressive countries or oppressive businesses. It's always darkest just before the revolution, so we can reasonably expect better results someday from a turnaround nation that was formerly repressive with high taxes and a top-down management style. Economies that are minimally repressive and support free trade and low taxes are likely to shine.

Modern slavery is a crime against humanity. Forced labor, forced marriage, sex slavery, harsh and deadly labor conditions and work for no pay will hold back a nation from achieving significant economic success. 12% of African women are married by 15 years old, according to a January 14, 2019, report by the World Economic Forum.

Early in the Industrial Revolution, child labor was the norm. Humans have improved but not enough. Between 30 and 50 million fellow humans are enslaved in the world today.

Government policies are continually changing. Policies that retard mankind's progress are rarely permanent. Oppressive taxation, regulation and laws, repression of freedom, women's rights, gay rights and free enterprise rarely succeed as national policy.

It is possible to mess this wonderful world up. It's also possible to change everything with one election or transformational government.

When it comes to investing, it's better to be an optimist. When the oppressors get the upper hand, revolution is sure to follow. It's always darkest just before dawn. Don't be a pessimistic investor.

The Final Word

When it comes to investing, it has almost always been appropriate to err on the side of progress, profit and technology. The pessimism of pauper investors will lead them to sell you their perfectly good investments at bargain prices.

This will typically occur when the media is reporting the worst possible news, convincing paupers that tragedy is right around the corner with little hope of recovery. You should always be skeptical of bad news.

A well-balanced portfolio of investments that adheres to sound modern portfolio theory will weather most economic storms. If you and your advisor have done your jobs, your risk should be under control. Don't be tempted to sell your good stuff at bargain-basement prices because of perceived bad news: that's the time to buy.

Chapter Six

Have a Financial Plan from Graduation to Retirement

Retirement didn't exist for our ancient ancestors. Disease and injury limited the average lifespan of our ancestral species to about 30 years. Those who survived past 15 had a shot at living to 60 years or more, however. The good news from your family tree is that almost all your ancestors made it past 15 or you wouldn't be here.

Recently I've been reading about the Paleo Diet, which is supposed to reduce type-2 diabetes, arthritis and other modern ailments. The human body starts to breakdown around age 60 without modern medicine.

Modern sedentary life is damaging to our health. *Younger Next Year* by Chris Crowley and Henry S. Lodge suggests that constant exercise can reverse the ravages of aging.

Cavemen and hunter gatherers lifted heavy things. They sprinted and walked constantly for survival and the whole time they were barefooted. Cavemen and hunter gatherers ate natural foods and meats and got plenty of sunshine.

Cavemen often fasted. They hunted and gathered ceaselessly. Subsistence living and surviving didn't allow for much leisure time.

There's evidence that ancient cultures honored their elder members. Abraham was certainly the esteemed elder leader of his family. While those who became senior citizens were revered, they couldn't enjoy retirement as we can today. With proper planning, we are likely to have both wealth and good health in retirement.

The concept of retirement is a relatively new notion. The Roman legions were among the first to have retirement. After 16 to 26 years of marching and fighting, a centurion could typically retire with Roman citizenship, a monthly pension and a plot of land[28].

In 1883, Bismarck's Germany set 65 as the probable age of retirement due to work incapacity[29]. In 1930 America, the average life expectancy was 58 for men and 62 for women. Social Security set 65 as the date seniors could begin taking their benefits. Retirement wasn't expected to last very long back then.

Retirement remained a privilege of the rich until recent times. If you were born to the right family, you rarely had to get your hands dirty. Servants took care of your needs. Retirement wasn't much different from the rest of your life.

Things started to change for the average American around 1950. Life expectancies began to improve and continue to do so with a little exception due to Covid19. Today, a married couple has a 60 percent probability that one of them will make it to age 90.[30].

Americans 65 and older are the fastest-growing age group, and the U. S. Administration on Aging projects there will be 72 million of us over 65 by 2030.

It's important to save for retirement. If your only source of income is Social Security, it's likely to be a meager retirement. One-third of retired households have Social Security as their only income[31].

According to ssa.gov, the social security website, in June 2022 there were over 70 million recipients of SSI and Supplemental Security Income. The average income per recipient was $18,506.64 per year and less for the disabled and survivors.

This statistic alone could motivate a future retiree to save more and start earlier. According to Wikipedia, the Social Security Trust

Fund had $2.908 trillion dollars and is projected to deplete by 2034. Without changes, payroll taxes will likely cover 76% of the current payments and increases after depletion.

Adjustments are likely to occur that will extend full retirement from 67 years old to 69 or later for most retirees. Current retirees and those close to retirement will likely not be affected.

Having 70 million recipients of SSI is a stabilizing economic factor and makes us less likely to have deep recessions like the Great Depression. Social Security recipients spend it all which stimulates the economy.

Your biggest expense in retirement will likely be healthcare. Most Americans could have difficulty affording retirement were it not for Medicare. Rising health care costs can cripple any budget as we age.

Medicare is projected to be solvent until 2026 by a September 2021 report by The American Hospital Association. This is why retirees have experienced rising Medicare premiums in recent years.

One in eight Americans over 65 is believed to have Alzheimer's, according to the Alzheimer's Association. One in four is thought to have diabetes, according to the Diabetes Association. Thirty two percent of Social Security recipients are considered obese.

Even with all these aliments, people are living longer due to modern medicine and better nutrition. Not long ago, people commonly died from consumption, diarrhea, vitamin deficiency, and even tooth decay.

According to the U.S. Administration on Aging, among people over age 65:

- 10 percent are smokers; 55 percent of men and 31 percent of women are former smokers.

- The average time spent watching TV is 4.1 hours a day.

- One person in 4 over 65 has at least one limitation in bathing, dressing, eating, walking or using the toilet.

If you are healthy and 65 or older, you should plan on living past age 90. Why not plan on living past 100? In The average American 65-years-old is expected to live to the ripe old age of 86.6 according to the 2022 Social Security Administration's life expectancy calculator.

If you never smoked, are active, continuing to work, have good teeth, garden, play a musical instrument, attend live musical concerts, speak a foreign language, interact with your grandchildren daily, and go to church you might make it to 100.

If you smoke, drink alcohol daily, skydive, deep sea dive, regularly drive a motorcycle, don't go to church, live alone, are homeless or have been arrested, your life expectancy is reduced.

Some professions have lower life expectancies. Suicide rates are higher among medical doctors, dentists, police officers, veterinarians, financial services, real estate agents, electricians and lawyers. Veterans are 2.5 times more likely to commit suicide than the average adult in America.

But if you have better than average longevity genes, medical science and better nutrition could extend your lifespan by decades. Why not be optimistic? Retirement failures have happened more often because of living longer than the average American.

Preparing for Retirement

Paupers say things like, "I'll never retire. I'll work 'til I drop." But you should have been preparing for retirement from your first job.

Even if you didn't, begin now to put away the proper amount into a retirement plan. You can dependably retire when you wish with an income that will maintain your standard of living.

If you were to save 10 percent of your salary from your first real job after graduation until normal retirement age of 67, you will have saved enough. You still must invest in a quality, balanced portfolio. Set goals that outpaces inflation and provides a stock market rate of return with the appropriate amount of risk.

In America the average household income in 2022 is $87,864 according to Zippia.com. The median income is $61,937. Your family's 10% savings should be enough.

If at age 25 you start investing $6,000 a year in an IRA buying a balanced securities portfolio earning 7 percent deferred annually, you could retire 42 years later with $1,480,658 according to my smart compounding calculator. This factors in an inflation rate so we are talking about close to today's dollars.

If the rate of return is closer to the historic 10% stock market rate of return, the number is astounding. That 25-year-old would have $3,548,404.

The younger investor could have a more aggressive balanced portfolio that could yield even more than 10%. Avoid just one of the average 9 bear markets and an average balanced portfolio will be up 10% more.

Every deposit going into a quality retirement plan would reduce the income of the investor and save taxes. The young investor really has the benefit of having the IRS contributing about 20% of each deposit that would instead go to withholding.

Should you receive and just spend your total salary? You would be making the IRS very happy.

Saving early in your working career is more important than saving later. Theoretically, if a 35-year-old worker contributed $10,037 a year to a retirement plan earning 10% annually during their working career until age 67 and nothing more until retirement, they would have saved $2,220,894. The total investment would be 32 X $10,037 or $321,184.

If the same earner started 10 years earlier at age 25 and invested $6,000 a year for 10 years and never put in another penny, his total investment would be $60,000. His compounded retirement fund at age 67 would be the same $2,220,894.

Numbers don't lie. Would you rather have a retirement plan that cost you $60,000 or one that cost you $321,184?

Don't forget this amount could be tax free. If our earner and saver choose to save in a Roth IRA, which is an after-tax investment, there would be no tax savings. After 5 years or age 59 ½, the saver could get the money and the gains out income tax free.

To participate, a person must have a job and earn a wage. The maximum contribution each year under current rules is $6,000 or $7,000 if over age 50.

There's talk that the Social Security Administration is bankrupt, but I believe it's likely to be there for you with some minor modifications. Full retirement age is 67 for anyone born in 1960 or later. If Social Security makes changes, your full retirement age might be a year or two past 67.

Payroll contributions for employers and employees alike might have to be increased. For paupers, Social Security is likely to account for 50 to 100 percent of their income. For you, it should represent less than 30 percent, not because you aren't going to get it but because you've saved enough.

The most common age to start Social Security payments is still 62 but is dropping every year. Each year you delay SSI your check increases 6.7% to 8% until you reach age 70. There are reasons to start your plan that make sense at every age. There are excellent SSI calculators available online that will estimate your best options.

My math brain says it's better to delay taking it early, especially if you are still working and in good health. There are no government guarantee investment accounts giving you 6.7% to 8% risk free that I can find.

Poor health could be a reason to start early but your spouse's survivor benefit would go up every year you wait to start SSI. You would be getting a smaller check for the rest of your life and so will your spouse if you should pass away early in your 70s. If your check is the largest of the family, that replaces his or her smaller check.

Social Security is better than a pension as the cost-of-living adjustment or COLA is built into the calculations. Inflation was 5.9% in 2022 and 2023 is 8.7%.. The Social Security COLA is meant to keep up with inflation. The increases in Medicare premiums will be making that more difficult.

Pensions don't include cost of living increases for the most part. Fixed annuity payments also don't increase. As groceries or gas prices increase with inflation, put your confidence in your Social Security check going forward.

Let's say you retire. Your pension is $5,000 a month and inflation is 3 ½ % a year. Your buying power in 20 years would be eroded to $2,512 a month. You then might be faced with some hard decisions.

Those guaranteed payments where the investment company promises a lifetime 5% rate of return could be wrongheaded if your future buying power is decimated. I talk more about the realistic goal of having a rising income during your entire retirement in a future chapter.

Very few businesses and even government entities choose to offer pensions today. Consider yourself lucky if you are one of the few to have one.

You should still be saving outside of your retirement plan with non-qualified savings. Put aside a small amount from each paycheck in a savings account.

Your first goal for this savings account should be to set aside three to six month's income in an emergency fund. Other non-qualified income generally includes inheritances, gifts and personal property, such as the equity in your home. Having funds outside your retirement plan can help you retire earlier.

If you choose to retire before 59½, there's a nasty 10 percent IRS penalty on qualified before tax savings like 401ks, IRAs, and thrift savings plans.

You will likely have to pay taxes at your marginal tax rate, the highest tax rate. The combination of tax penalty and higher tax rate make it difficult to retire young if your only savings are qualified plans.

Non-qualified savings might solve the early retirement problem. Non-qualified savings can include real estate, savings accounts, money in your checking account, non-IRA annuities called non-qualified annuities, cash value life insurance and death benefits from life insurance, inheritances, gifts, and any other savings or wealth that isn't accumulated in a tax deferred government retirement plan.

If you have ever watched Antiques Roadshow, don't count out antiques, art or collectibles as a way of funding early retirement. Non-qualified savings have no 10% early-withdrawal penalty and may have preferential tax treatment. The original cost basis of a non-qualified investment likely won't be taxed when it is withdrawn. After reaching age 59½, all your retirement savings likely become accessible penalty-free but not tax free.

There are several ways of getting penalty-free money from a retirement plan, some of which I don't recommend. Your money is penalty free if you pass away or are permanently disabled. You can take penalty-free withdrawals from your 401k and certain other retirement plans without a 10 percent penalty if you are retired and over 55.

If you haven't saved in an emergency fund, you can normally borrow from you 401k. You can't borrow from an IRA. You can't pledge an IRA to a lender either.

You can borrow from cash value whole life insurance. You can't borrow from an annuity. Visit with a qualified tax professional before borrowing to avoid nasty penalties and tax surprises.

You cannot take penalty-free withdrawals from an IRA until age 59½. If you have a Roth IRA, you can withdraw your original investment without penalty.[32] You can withdraw your earnings penalty free after age 59½ plus five years. If you converted to a Roth, watch for that five-year mark to get the earnings out penalty free.

A Rising Income Your Whole Retirement

A rising income will likely be needed for a longer retirement. Take an example of two imaginary families, both spouses 62 years old with one spouse that didn't work. Imagine the year is 1998. The two families made different choices that could result in dramatically different outcomes.

Family A decided to take Social Security immediately at 62 in addition to the guaranteed income offered by the pension plan of the working spouse's employer. They now had a remarkable and generously comfortable income for 1998 of $3,100 a month. "That's enough for us to live comfortably our whole retirement. I like the guarantee and we can even save some," said Mr. A.

Family B elected a lump sum cash settlement from his pension plan. Our firm rolled this over into a Rollover IRA and invested in a balanced portfolio. It was a custodian-to-custodian rollover, so no taxes were due. Mr. B decided to delay SSI until full retirement age of 65. Mr. B also retired from his full-time job. He found a part-time job at an auto parts store to make up some of the temporary income difference.

Non-working spouses are entitled to one-half of their working spouse's Social Security benefit. Mr. A's wife took her 50% SSI at age 62. Mr. B's wife delayed taking SSI until age 65 and also took one half of Mr. B's check. Family B would be getting approximately 22% bigger Social Security checks than Family A for the rest of their lives.

Now let's fast forward both families to 2022.

Social Security COLA increases were more generous to Family B by 22%. Medicare increases have become a real drag for Family A as their smaller checks were reduced by a greater percentage.

Family A's pension check didn't increase so now income is tight and their budget is strained. The family continues to live on $3,100 per month.

Once family B started taking SSI at 65, Mr. B could cut back his part time job at the auto parts store. The balanced portfolio kept up with inflation and gave family B a rising income that along with their SSI is now $5,598 a month.

If Mr. A passes away in 2022, his pension stops and there aren't any survivor benefits. Mrs. A will get only the Social Security check and that will be Mr. A's age 62 check.

If Mr. B passes away in 2022, Mrs. B gets Mr. B's rollover IRA now over $854,000. That lump sum of $390,000 has been growing at approximately 4% per year while giving family B an income of roughly 4% per year and growing.

Mrs. B also gets Mr. B's SSI check that is 22% larger than Mr. A's check.

This imaginary situation is assuming a modest 8% growth rate, an inflation rate of 3% and a COLA of 3% on average. Editor required disclaimer: No year has ever been average. No one can predict the future earnings or future SSI payments. And even more importantly, no one can predict how long you will live.

During my career, I have witnessed more than one family that made similar decisions to Family A. During this period, many of these families ran short of funds and are now living on SSI alone.

I've witnessed many more families living on rising incomes, with excellent incomes like family B. The survivor benefits are clearly better with Family B.

Now that life expectancies are even longer, I suggest you consider delaying SSI to age 70 if possible. This decision can increase SSI to your family by as much as 85% or more compared to the 62 year-old reduced benefit. More about this in a later chapter.

The Balanced Portfolio

I've been talking about a balanced portfolio. What does one look like, you might ask? A balanced portfolio should have the appropriate mix of stock, fixed income and income producing real estate to achieve a competitive yield and reduced overall risk.

It might also include a small percentage of non-correlated assets: alternative investments, commodities, business development corporations, venture capital investments, undeveloped land, art, antiques and collectibles.

The balanced portfolio concept really started with Modern Portfolio Theory (MPT), first introduced by Harry Markowitz in 1952. Mr. Markowitz won a Noble Prize in 1990 in Economic Sciences.

MPT is a theory of how risk-averse investors can construct portfolios to optimize or maximize expected returns, based on a given level of market risk and emphasizing that risk is an inherent part of seeking a higher reward.

Harvard University expanded the concept of MPT to include non-correlated assets that can dramatically reduce the losses earlier balanced portfolios experienced during protracted bear markets in US stocks.

While the traditional portfolio had 60 percent stocks and 40 percent bonds, Harvard (and Yale) injected more real estate, better research, hedging, inflation-protected and alternative investments, and longer hold times that can span decades on some investments.

Harvard reduced its investment in stocks from 65 percent in 1980 to only about 20 percent during the past decade. Most of Harvard's investments yield income during the holding period.

The Harvard University endowment was valued at $53.4 billion as recently as June 4, 2022. Yale and University of Texas are not that far behind at around $42 billion each. These institutions are doing something right.

Average investors view alternative long-term investments as too risky. The Harvard Endowment theory of investing believes just the opposite, that they are less risky when held long term.

Average investors are unable to maintain a long-term view that spans decades unless they have lots of money and a generational wealth perspective. Investors whose families own significant land, oil and gas investments, valuable antiques, art or jewelry are more likely to hold a long-term view.

Work with your investment advisor and develop a plan to construct a balanced portfolio to meet your specific needs. Keep an open mind about investments that might not be familiar. These could be the investments that increase growth, yield a higher income and lower your long-term risk.

If your advisor suggests you put all your money into an insurance product with a hefty exit penalty, you should probably explore other options. That is not the balanced portfolio your family deserves.

Let's examine the building blocks that comprise a balanced portfolio. The stock portion of a balanced portfolio might include income-producing value stocks and growth stocks. There are also small-cap[33], mid-cap[34] and large-cap[35] stock value and growth categories to consider.

Each of these categories contains both domestic and foreign issues. Each classification of stock will behave differently and have different risks.

The following chart lists a range of asset percentages that should fit most investor needs. Each category is expressed as a percentage, with all categories and sub-categories adding up to 100 percent. For example, if you allocate 40 percent to stocks and 50 percent to large-cap growth stocks within that category, you would be putting 20 percent of your overall money into large-cap growth.

ASSET CATEGORY	% INVESTED	% OF TOTAL
STOCKS	**20-80**	
Small cap growth	5-15	3
Small cap value	10-20	5
Large cap growth	20-40	12
Large cap value	30-50	20
International	20-40	10
REAL ESTATE	**0-30**	
Income producing	0-100	15
Individually owned	0-100	
Undeveloped land	0-100	
FIXED INCOME	**20-80**	
Taxable bonds	0-50	10 **
Tax-free bonds	0-100	10 **
Convertible bonds	0-20	5
Preferred stocks	0-20	5
Senior floating rate bonds/notes	0-20	5
Inflation protected bonds	0-50	5
Mortgage backed investments	0-40	5
ALTERNATIVE INVESTMENTS*	**0-30**	
Oil & gas	0-100	
Commodities	0-50	
Managed futures	0-50	
Volatility index	0-20	
Hedged investments	0-100	
Precious metals	0-100	
Collectibles, art, antiques	0-100	
Cash value life insurance	0-100	

* Be certain you are knowledgeable about alternative investments before investing. You can lose your entire investment in many alternative investments and in some cases, lose more than you invested.

** One or the other account. Taxable bonds should be placed in a Qualified account: Tax-free bonds should be placed in a Non-Qualified account.

In general, small-cap growth stocks and emerging-market foreign stocks[36] have higher risk than large-cap growth or value stocks. Small-cap stocks are usually less stable companies that are at greater risk of failure than established larger companies. Small-cap stocks may often grow faster but must borrow more money and are more vulnerable to competition.

Real estate comes in many different categories. If you own your home, you likely have a significant investment in real estate. Since your residence won't produce an income, it generally is excluded from balanced portfolio calculations.

Real estate can be either developed or undeveloped. Developed real estate is likely to yield an income that can contribute to your overall retirement check. Real-estate income can make a significant contribution to growing your portfolio over time.

Undeveloped real estate is likely to require expenses to develop, long holding times, lack income, and have higher risks and payoffs than developed real estate.

If you own one rental property in one market in one category with one lessee, you have high risk. If you have a diversified portfolio of real estate across many markets with many lessees in multiple categories, you have lower risk.

Real estate is illiquid. It can take years or even decades before an investor can sell with a profit. Owners of individual properties are susceptible to investment risk: expenses, depreciation, taxes, insurance and maintenance can all reduce the bottom line. Real estate can offer tax advantages because of depreciation and repair expense deductions.

Leverage or borrowing money on real estate increases risk, but, when done well, can increase income on properties. Leverage is not innately positive or negative but should be considered when buying any real estate investment.

The fixed income category includes a variety of investments: government, corporate and foreign government bonds, bank deposits and certificates of deposits, preferred stocks, convertible bonds, mortgages, municipal or tax-free bonds, and senior floating-rate investments among them.

Bonds come in short, medium and long durations. Credit worthiness ranges from highest rated AAA to investment grade, high yield or junk grade and default grade. In general, highest rated short duration bonds pay the lowest interest rates, and longer-duration, lower-rated bonds pay a higher interest rate.

Bonds have interest-rate risk. When interest rates change, bonds either gain or lose value. If interest rates rise, bonds generally lose value. The highest-quality, longest-duration[37] bonds lose the most value.

Lower-quality bonds lose value most when default risk increases due to economic conditions. Short- duration bonds yield lower rates of return. There is also inflation risk—the risk that a bond's yield and principal will buy less goods and services at maturity due to rates of return that are lower than inflation.

As previously mentioned, alternative investments, hedging, commodities, business development corporations, venture capital investments, undeveloped land, art, antiques, and collectibles can have a place in the modern balanced portfolio. Most IRAs or retirement plans can't hold such assets unless held as a marketable security.

A balanced portfolio should experience less volatility. Some investments go up while other investments go down. Your goal might be to never take withdrawals, to reinvest all dividends and to double your investment with reasonable risk. You are unlikely to reach your goal during your lifetime with a guaranteed principal investment that compounds at 1 to 3 percent a year. It would take 24 to 70 or so years to reach your goal.

With the current higher inflation rate, buying power would be reduced much more than the guaranteed return. The most important part of investing is being able to buy more gas and groceries during your whole retirement.

If you owned an investment that dependably had 6 percent income reinvested, you could reach your goal and double your investment in 12 years, even if the underlying investment appreciated at 0 percent each year. If your investment paid 6 percent income AND appreciated at 6 percent each year, you would double your money in an astounding 6 years.

It's logical to lower your risk if you are approaching or in retirement. Remember, you are likely to be retired for 20 to 40 years.

Younger investors can hold more small-cap stocks, undeveloped real estate, technology stocks, high-yield bonds and emerging-market foreign investments.

Older or retired investors might do better with value stocks, income-producing real estate, emerging-market infrastructure and utility investments, and tax-free bonds.

If you have a double dose of the fear gene, train yourself to invest when markets are down. When stock prices are down, your risk is lower.

If you are a fearful investor, a lower-risk, balanced portfolio that gives you a reasonable and dependable income stream can provide comfort: the original investment might fluctuate but your dividend income remains constant or grows.

Another way to reduce risk when initially investing is called Dollar Cost Averaging (DCA). Dollar cost averaging into investments from a less-risky position involves moving a set percentage of the low-risk or risk-free investment into a stock market, real estate or higher-risk bond or fixed income position. An example of DCA-ing would be contributing regularly to a 401k or IRA.

Let's say that we have $100,000 to invest and we are not certain today is a good time to invest. What if we invested $20,000 today into a balanced portfolio and then invested the same amount each month over the next 4 months on the same day of the month until the whole amount is invested?

If the stock market were to have a correction or drop in value during the 5 months, you would be getting the lower prices and therefore, would buy more shares during the dip.

What if, on the other hand, stocks and the other components of the balanced portfolio went up? The original purchases would then appreciate. You can reduce your risk by DCA-ing. And you can gain peace of mind by knowing that you are likely to have a lower-risk result, whatever happens.

DCA investments don't guarantee that you will have a positive result. When the signs are looking like there is likely a recession starting, delay the start of the DCA plan. Just let those paupers bid down their valuable stuff until the selloff is well underway.

Grow your investments with stock dividends, interest from bank investments, bond coupon income and occasional appreciation. You can enjoy a long, happy retirement with lower-risk investments.

It's easy for me to tell you to stop that pauper side of your brain from thinking. It's easier to just accept that you are a conservative investor.

Develop a plan to build a balanced portfolio that's within your risk budget and feel comfortable with the risks you are taking. In the long run, your returns might be slightly lower than with a higher-risk balanced portfolio, but your peace of mind is important too.

I recommend you take a disciplined investment approach that allows you to hold a range of investments. I tend to recommend lowering exposure to an asset class when the stock, bond or real estate market is high and raising exposure to the same asset class when that market is in correction.

Put another way, buy stocks, bonds, real estate and alternative investments while they are low, and sell them while they are high. Paupers buy high and sell low. If you are still resistant, reread chapter one.

You now are ready to write an investment policy statement (IPS). According to fi360, the global fiduciary standard of excellence, there are 21 questions to ask in a self-assessment that can determine whether you are taking care of your responsibilities. Most individuals don't want to go that far, but the full standards are available on the fi360 website. Here are the components of a good IPS:

- How will you engage and discharge advisors and other professionals?

- Who will make the decisions for the portfolio? Are they competent? If not competent, is there a durable power of attorney for a competent person to manage the portfolio?

- Are there conflicts of interest between the advisor, custodian and owner?

- Are the portfolio assets protected against theft and embezzlement?

- Have you established an investment time horizon?

- Have you established an appropriate risk level for your portfolio?

- What is the expected rate of return for the portfolio?

- Are you able to monitor your investments?

- Have you selected potential appropriate asset classes?

- Is a reasonable due-diligence process followed to select your investment advisor, custodian and asset class providers?

- Are easily understood portfolio reports readily available?

- Are periodic reviews arranged to compare your results to your objectives?

- Are there periodic reviews of trading practices and proxy voting, investment related expenses and compensation of advisors?

- Are the tax consequences of the investments considered?

- Are your investments liquid? Are there excessive exit penalties should you need your money back?

As you can see, this can get a little cumbersome. I hope this partial list will help you ask the right questions before you invest.

Once or twice a year, your portfolio should be rebalanced back to your original percentages. This will usually result in selling high and buying low since everything sold normally will be higher and everything bought normally will be lower. You could also rebalance with new contributions.

Depending on your objectives and circumstances, an ideal portfolio might include risk. You will benefit from balancing the risk you are willing to accept with the return you are hoping to receive. You can lower risk by investing in principal-guaranteed investments, but these may have a subpar rate of return.

The next step is to see what your current portfolio looks like. If you have everything in one bucket, get to work. You need to reallocate your portfolio.

Retirement Challenges

You should be able to retire when you want to retire. The only thing holding you back would be that the younger person you once were didn't save enough. You should have had a talk with your younger self and expressed your desire to retire at 55.

If you planned on a 20-year retirement when you were young, you can now assume that retirement could be 30 years or longer. That adds another 10 years of uncertainty. If you are exceptionally healthy, you might add another decade or two to that projection. What are the possibilities that you will be unable to retire and more importantly, stay retired?

A big risk is inflation, or more precisely, cost-of-living increases. During the two decades 1993 to 2013, the annual inflation rate averaged about 2.4 percent. The previous two decades before saw inflation rates as high as 13.5 percent.

Can we agree that 3 percent is a conservative rate of inflation going forward? To keep pace, your income would need to double every 20 to 24 years. That means you can't rely on guaranteed investments that yield 1 to 3 percent a year and expect to stay retired...unless you have millions.

Recent spikes in inflation are making retirement planning even more challenging. The 2022 Cost of Living Adjustment or COLA was 5.9% for all SSI recipients. This took effect in January 2022. Current estimates for the 2023 COLA are 8.7%.

A study indicated retirees in 1999 were asking for an annual withdrawal rate of 8 to 10 percent[38]. Economists at the time advised that withdrawing 5 percent was a wiser option, as it would allow accounts to grow at a rate to match inflation.

This would increase the number of dollars retirees received each year but would merely sustain their standard of living and nothing more, because of the inflationary effect.

With today's low rates of return on fixed-income, principal-guaranteed investments, a 3 percent annual withdrawal is thought to be the sustainable rate.[39] The fear going forward is that the fixed portion of your retirement nest egg might not carry as much water for you as in previous years. That means you may need to save more during your working years in order to stay retired with a growing income.

To illustrate the impact of inflation, let's consider a 25-year- old who begins saving for retirement by making her maximum IRA contribution of $6,000 annually. Incidentally, that contribution would also reduce her taxable income and her taxes each year.

Let's assume her account was invested in a balanced portfolio that earned 8 percent compounded annually. At age 67—the Social Security current full-retirement age—she would have a staggering $1,971,498 for retirement.

Of course, those would be inflated dollars. The purchasing power equivalent of when she began saving at age 25 would be $851,960. Her distributions are likely to be taxable, but at a lower tax rate than during her working years.

IRAs are infested with taxes. The cure is to convert to a Roth IRA. Uncle Sam wants 12 to 37% of everything in a traditional IRA and nothing in a Roth. If you are likely to have an equal or higher tax rate at retirement, plan for a Roth conversion or invest in Roth IRAs from the beginning.

If instead, that 25-year-old saved in a Roth IRA, that money would be tax free in retirement, adding a significant additional income to Social Security—income she doesn't have to share with Uncle Sam. While no one knows what tax-law changes will take place over the next 40 years, it's unlikely that her SSI would fall beneath the threshold so that it also would be tax free.

What might derail this retirement super train? The same few pitfalls that can derail any financial plan. I'm excluding global events beyond our control. Here's the short list of obstacles you can exercise some control over:

1.   Debt and excessive spending

2.   Retiring too early

3.   Divorce and family problems

4.   Illness, disability, addiction and premature death

5.   Unemployment

6.   Unwise investment choices

7.   Excess taxation

In a perfect world, everyone would have a good education, be in good health, have a loving family, a rewarding career, live within their means and avoid debt. No one would fall prey to fraudulent investments, and their balanced portfolios would yield the perfect average growth rate every year.

Unfortunately, we don't live in a perfect world, and real life happens on a much-too-frequent basis. It's essential to avoid making unwise decisions that can make it almost impossible to get back on track. There are many books on this very subject.

Debt and Excessive Spending

Pauper brains think they have more wealth if they spend more money. They believe having the newest car, biggest house or best clothes make them wealthy. Paupers often congregate at country clubs, jewelry and clothing stores and expensive restaurants.

The truly wealthy can also be found at such places but often drive an older vehicle and avoid ostentatious displays of their wealth. There's a saying: "I didn't get wealthy by wasting my money." The wealthy hate debt; paupers are submerged in it.

While a good education can make all the difference in a young person's future, a smothering student loan can offset much of the advantage. Paupers tend to borrow to go to school. I suppose it's a way to pass the pauper legacy on to the next generation. My advice to young people is to cash flow an education if you or your parents couldn't save enough.

Choose an affordable school with quality academics and ask for the job placement ratio for your major. You do want to be able to get a job after you graduate.

Trade schools and technical schools are a great alternative to a traditional 4 year—or in my case 5 year—education at a private or state university. If a student finds a rewarding profession, he or she can often make more income than a college graduate. The bonus is they are getting on the job training and experience while getting a quality education.

Many community colleges have programs connected to local high schools that will allow for a low cost or free Associates Degree. A 4-year university will then transfer the credits and your family just saved $50,000 or more in student loans.

The pauper brain tells you to buy a shiny new car. Math says this is one of the worst decisions that you can make. Cars are consumables. Most end up worthless. The first day you own a new car cost you between 5 and 15 percent of the purchase price.

This depreciation continues by as much as 25 percent in the first year. Let the paupers buy new cars. My advice is to buy a nice car within your budget that is 3 to 5 years old with reasonable mileage.

If your budget is tight, buy a dimpled darling that sells at a meaningful discount and runs well. Pay cash for the car. Make large payments and pay off the car within a year if you can't pay cash. Do all of this within your budget. Basic transportation shouldn't be a financial burden.

Paupers hate budgets. Paupers spend more than they earn. They buy what they want without thinking of consequences. Paupers have high-interest-rate credit cards with carry-over balances that they use a lot. It is a very poor way to live. My recommendation is to create a budget and live within it.

The day of low interest on mortgages may be over. A homeowner that has a 30-year mortgage pays a significantly higher interest rate than a homeowner with a 15- or 20-year mortgage. 20 years ago, my wife and I did a 5-year mortgage and paid only 4% when 30-year mortgages were around 9 percent a year.

With a lower mortgage rate, we then directed our savings efforts to paying off the house. We've had a mortgage-free house for the last 25 years. We then directed our efforts to saving for retirement. Amazing how easy budgeting is when there's no mortgage payment.

If your home mortgage is paid, you don't owe on credit cards, you drive a nice but modest dependable car and live within your budget, you will likely have a more successful retirement.

Retiring Too Early

In a recent Bankrate survey,[40] three quarters of American workers said they expect to continue working after retirement. Most enjoyed work and would miss it should they retire cold turkey. Working past retirement age is a great way to get the most out of every dollar you've saved.

You could also choose to delay SSI until as late as age 70. Every year you delay retirement, your investments grow. You contribute more to those investments, and Social Security payments increase by as much as 8 percent a year for the rest of your life. Social Security is the only income for about 28 percent of retirees but could almost double if left untouched until age 70.

The calculation is much too complicated to be definitive, but if your only choices were to retire at 62 and take SSI or work until 70 without activating your SSI, you could likely get about double your age 62 income at age 70.

It would take only until about age 79½ to 82 to have received the same total payments as your 62-year-old "retired-on-the- first-day-possible" self. From 79½ to 82 to when you pass away, your income would be doubled. If you are in excellent health and live a long life into your 90s, the math is overwhelming in your favor to delay SSI.

You can continue to chuck money into your IRA, 401k, and non-qualified savings nest eggs. Your retirement and savings can double during the same time with just normal growth and contributions. That modest retirement becomes a supersized, fulfilling retirement. You were planning on living longer after retirement anyway, so why not have twice as much money?

SSI also has the Cost-of-Living Allowance or COLA feature that is meant to keep up with inflation. Medicare premiums are deducted from your SSI payment and go up with inflation. Many recipients of SSI complain that the Medicare increases consumed all their SSI COLA. This is much less likely when your check is super-sized.

A 70-year-old SSI recipient will get much more beneficial COLA than a 62-year-old recipient. The COLA for 2022 was 5.9% and 2023 estimates are over 8.7%. Medicare premiums are fixed for every recipient.

You must take SSI by age 70. You may want to continue saving in your own retirement plan if you continue to work. The math works in your favor to save past 70. You now can make deductible IRA payments after 70 if you or your spouse have earned income.

You can continue to put money into your 401k or most other large, employer-sponsored retirement plans. In most cases, you don't have to take out required minimum distributions (RMD) at 72 as long as you are working.

Roth IRAs have long allowed contributions after age 70 if you or your spouse have earned income. Earned income usually is from a job with FICA withholding. A CPA or accountant can also let you know if your individually owned business will allow you to make deductible contributions to an IRA. There are no tax saving deductions from income allowed for Roths.

Roth IRAs don't require you to take RMDs during your lifetime. If you inherit your spouse's Roth IRA due to his or her death, it can become your Roth IRA. You may keep it tax free, just as if you had made the contributions.

As long as you have earned income, you can contribute to a Roth IRA[41]. You can also contribute to your non-working spouse's Roth. In 2022, the amount is $6,000 each or $12,000 per couple per year, or $7,000 each or$14,000 for couples over 50. In 2023, the amount is $6,500 each or $13,000 per couple per year, or $7,700 each or $15,000 for couples over 50.

Roth IRAs are an attractive asset to inherit. What's there not to like about tax free? Most life insurance death benefits are tax free. Taxes get tricky with annuities. These assets pass probate free in almost all cases by simply presenting a death certificate and filing a transfer request.

Annuities that are non-qualified or non-retirement annuities have complicated tax consequences when you turn on the withdrawals. Retirement annuities are taxable according to IRA, 403b, Roth or other rules. Individually owned annuities will tax withdrawals of all gains as ordinary income until the owner reaches the cost basis. Cost basis withdrawals from non-qualified annuities are tax free.

Traditional inherited IRAs have complicated RMD requirements. I recommend that you work with a qualified tax professional or financial planner to determine how to avoid steep penalties. Spouses are allowed to roll over inherited IRAs into their name. Non-spouses fall under a five-year rule or a ten-year rule and must take RMDs.

Divorce and Family Problems

I'm sure our ancient ancestors had family problems. Ever since monogamy became all the rage, we've been bickering with our spouses. Different cultures handle divorce and family problems in a variety of ways. Let's talk about how we handle them in modern America.

Your divorced spouse is entitled to 50 percent of your business, your house, your car and your personal belongings. They really mean it when they say splitting the sheets. The biggest fight can be over the kids and perhaps the dog. How are you supposed to split the dog? I saw a custody agreement where each spouse was given visitation for the dog.

In most states the spouse gets 50 percent of the retirement plan accumulated during the marriage. If a couple has accumulated two equal retirement plans, it's relatively easy to divide the accounts.

Paupers tend to marry for the wrong reasons and to marry other paupers. That can be a disastrous union. Competitive spending is often a sport in a pauper household, which of course would have negative consequences at retirement.

If done correctly, separate property you own when you marry can continue to be separate property after divorce. Ask your financial and legal team of professionals to protect your separate property. If comingled, separate property becomes community property.

Inherited property, contributions to retirement plans before marriage, real estate individually owned by one or the other spouse, and gifts from a loved one are likely separate property.

Almost everything else is not separate property. This can vary greatly from state to state, so consult professionals familiar with your state's laws. Usually, income from separate property is community property and therefore owned equally by both spouses.

I recommend you increase your chances of marrying the right person by attending premarital counseling from a qualified specialist. Many cities have counseling services that specialize in helping a young couple get off on the right foot.

If you would like some easy reading on how to budget, how to discuss financial issues with your new spouse, and other important issues, go to the Suggested Reading List at the end of the book.

Illness and Disability

Even in ancient times, youth thought they were indestructible. Wars have always been fought by the young. They have quicker reflexes but also less fear of the consequences. As we approach retirement, I'm pretty sure that our bodies are letting us know things aren't the same.

When we are young, we think we will live forever and never get sick. Paupers often extend that assumption long into adulthood. Medical expenses can be devastating to a financial plan.

At 65, most Americans qualify for Medicare, which in many cases, is more important than SSI. For the elderly, medical expense will overwhelm any budget. Medicare covers that need at a reasonable cost.

Without health insurance, disability insurance and eventually long-term care insurance, your estate and retirement plan can be eviscerated by anything more serious than a trivial illness. Everyone gets sick. Some become so ill they can no longer care for their own maintenance and daily living activities. With medical-science assistance, a debilitating illness can last for years.

Long term chronic health conditions now being successfully treated include but are not limited to diabetes, cardiovascular and heart disease, chronic kidney disease, chronic respiratory illnesses, chronic neurological illnesses like multiple sclerosis, chronic pain, autoimmune diseases, mental illness and addiction. Our ancient ancestors were unable to deal with these issues. Life expectancy could be short if your ancient ancestors even had dental problems.

If you should become ill or disabled during your working career, your family is hit with a double whammy. In addition to the expense of the illness, you now don't have an income from work.

Your spouse may find it difficult or impossible to work, particularly if he or she must take care of you. If you die at a young age or "out of order," you will leave your family with debts and no means of maintaining their lifestyle.

The pauper says, "I don't want to think about it. My spouse will just waste the money on a new spouse." This is shortsighted thinking for those who purport to love their spouse and family.

If you are insurable, I recommend you purchase 7 to 15 times your annual salary in low-cost term insurance. If you are uninsurable, buy a similar amount or maximum amount from your employer's group coverage, if available. Group life coverage rarely requires you prove insurability.

If you are insurable, buy term insurance that is underwritten while you are in excellent health as soon as you have family obligations. I generally advise clients to buy the longest-term coverage possible for their age. It costs more, but the premiums remain fixed for up to 20 to 30 years.

If you smoke or use tobacco products, your insurance will cost about twice as much. I recommend that you go ahead and buy the appropriate amount of coverage and then quit smoking.

Once you are tobacco free, go back and reapply. You can get a big reduction in cost. After the new policy is issued you can drop the expensive coverage.

Most of the time, when applying for life insurance, you will qualify for standard rates unless you have significant health problems or are obese. If your height and weight, blood chemistry, family history and health are above average, you can qualify for preferred rates. Some carriers even have super preferred, preferred smoker and other ways of attracting the more desirable clients. If you qualify, ask for the best rates, more coverage, and longer terms.

While you are still working, if you qualify, you should consider purchasing disability insurance (DI). It will replace 60 to 70 percent of your income. DI is expensive, and underwriting is difficult, but it's especially important for professionals who spent years and sometimes fortunes on education.

If you are unable to perform your occupation, your payments will begin and usually continue for 2, 5, 10 years or until retirement, depending on the policy and riders you made at purchase. Again, you should apply early. You must be in excellent health to get decent rates.

Social Security also has disability insurance. You must be severely disabled and unable to perform any job. The fact that you can no longer be a lawyer, doctor or accountant won't get you DI income from Social Security. You must be unable to do anything.

The biggest expense you are likely to have will be custodial care in the last years of your life. Custodial care is usually provided by a nursing home, a professional caregiver in the home, or by a family member.

Long term care insurance (LTCI) starts when you can no longer perform the activities of daily living.[42] If you would like to get the latest statistics, go to the U.S. Department of Health and Human Services website at longtermcare.gov.

A recent Morningstar article stated that 70% of all nursing home residents are women. 80 is the average age of admission to a nursing home. Most women are the primary care giver for their spouses, who may also need nursing home coverage, to stay at home longer.

I recommend that you consider purchasing long term care coverage sometime while you are healthy between ages 55 and 65. Your LTCI out-of-pocket expense will likely approximate the total amount of the annual premiums paid to age 85, no matter when you start.

At age 55, the policy premiums for a couple might be $3,000 a year. That adds up to about $90,000 in premiums by age 85. Waiting until age 65 increases the premiums to around $4,800 a year, making the total cost at age 85 about $96,000.

If you bought the coverage at 55, you would have 10 extra years of coverage and save roughly $6,000. As you are much more likely to get a better rating at age 55, I recommend you buy LTCI coverage early if you can afford it.

Ways to reduce the costs include spousal discounts if both spouses apply, taking lower amounts of coverage with inflation protection, and buying partnership eligible plans if your state endorses such coverage.

Partnership plans may allow you to become eligible immediately for Medicaid coverage after your LTCI policy has paid its last payment without requiring the complete spend down to $2,000. If done correctly, this will protect all or a portion of a modest estate.

Long term care insurance is expensive. Some coverage is better than no coverage, but don't buy too much coverage. This is a complicated subject. Most CERTIFIED FINANCIAL PLANNER™ Practitioners can quote long term care coverage or can recommend a competent insurance professional in your area. Go to www.CFP.com and get a list of professionals in your area.

Unemployment

Unemployment is a relatively recent concept. Our ancient ancestors inherited the family business. As long as there was game on the savannah and roots, grains, fruit and berries to collect, all was well. Once agriculture began to transform our way of life, men and women became specialists.

One family would do better raising goats, another better making tools. They could then trade, and both families were better off. Wealth was created.

In modern times, unemployment is always a possibility. The wise person has an emergency fund to cover 3 to 6 months of expenses. If both spouses work, it can be less. Paupers tend to have debt and not save.

Federal Unemployment Insurance benefit coverage helps but isn't all that great. If you quit or are fired for just cause, you won't get anything. I recommend that you put away a sufficient emergency fund in low-risk, liquid investments with a high-quality bank custodian.

I should not need to say this, but you should slash discretionary spending and conserve your resources until your income is restored. Paupers tend go into denial and keep spending to keep up appearances. An emergency fund can last a long time when only the essentials are being paid.

Unwise Investment Choices

Paupers tend to view investments as a series of gambles. If they have had good luck with investments, they will take too much risk. If they have had bad luck, they will take no risk. Both approaches are wrong. Too much risk and investments can be wiped out or decimated during a normal market correction. Too little risk and investment earnings can be minimal or below the inflation rate.

Your objective is to invest in a diversified portfolio that contains an ample portion of investments with low correlations. That will help maximize your yield and reduce your risk.

Modern Portfolio Theory is a mathematical formulation of the concept of diversification in investing, with the aim of selecting a collection of investment assets that has collectively lower risk than any individual asset. This is possible, in theory, because different types of assets often change in value in opposite ways.

According to the Modern Portfolio Theory or MPT, it's possible to construct an efficient frontier of optimal portfolios offering the maximum possible expected return for a given level of risk.[43] The ultimate goal is to lower the risk and increase the yields using a balanced portfolio.

Paupers invest by instinct. Behaviors of fear, greed and gambling rule. Savvy investors know that a disciplined balanced portfolio can yield a reasonable return for a given level of risk exposure. Throw in an aversion to inflation and a desire to reduce taxes, and the results are apt to improve.

Several great books on building a quality balanced portfolio are included in the Reading List at the end of the book. If you choose to manage your own funds, I recommend you weigh your choice carefully. The book's concluding chapter has some valuable knowledge to consider before taking on the arduous task of portfolio self-management.

I recommend that you work with a CFP® professional, CERTIFIED FINANCIAL PLANNER™ Practitioner or Registered Investment Advisor with 5 or more years of experience. You want a seasoned financial professional that will act as your fiduciary.

A fiduciary duty is a legal duty to act solely in another party's interests. Fiduciaries may not profit from their relationship with their principals or clients unless they have the principals' express informed consent.

They also have a duty to avoid any conflicts of interest between themselves and their principals or between their principals and the fiduciaries' other clients. A fiduciary duty is the strictest duty of care recognized by the US legal system.[44] If I were you, I would demand this of all my financial professionals.

Most insurance brokers are not held to the fiduciary standard. They might provide you with an appropriate investment portfolio, but the critical suitability standard is lower.

Fiduciaries are required to disclose all material facts, whereas insurance agents must follow the business rules enacted by their state and in general are expected to act responsibly and ethically.

Fiduciaries are obligated to provide a balanced presentation; others are permitted to give a sales presentation. Here's a side-by-side comparison.

Fiduciary Standard versus Fair Dealing Standard

Fiduciary	Fair Dealing
Principles and relationship based	Rules and transaction based
Singular duty of loyalty	Divided loyalty
Due care of a prudent expert	Deal fairly, consistent with industry standards
Utmost good faith	Suitability
Avoid or manage conflicts	Conflicts may exist, unmanaged and undisclosed
Disclose material facts	Disclose certain material facts

Your goal should always be to receive advice and place investments that are in the best interest of your family. Requiring an advisor that has fiduciary responsibility increases the likelihood that you will get good advice. Taking advice from an untrained or inexperienced salesperson increases the likelihood that you will have a bad result.

Excess Taxation

In a perfect world, we would pay little or no taxes. Obviously, we do not live in a perfect world. The highest federal tax brackets have been rising and are currently 37 percent. Exemptions phase out for individuals with incomes above $539,000 and couples at $1,079,800 under current law.

State income taxes can be as high as 13.3% as they are in California or zero as they are in Texas. Roth IRAs held for 5 years or longer allow for tax-free distributions after the age of 59 ½ years old that are both state and federally tax free.

I think it is therefore important to note that some retirees will pay their last tax bill the year they retire. Do these retirees live a meager life? Not at all. They enjoy the same lifestyle as other retirees.

How then can they retire on good incomes and not pay taxes, you might ask? Are they cheating the government? Are they likely to be the targets of constant audits by the IRS? Again, not at all. They can retire without taxes because they planned during their working years to retire without taxes.

Let's consider how they do it. Social Security is taxable if your income is above certain limits. If you are married filing jointly and make over $32,000 MAGI,[45] up to 50 percent of your SSI could be taxable.

If you two rich folks make over $44,000 MAGI then up to 85 percent of your SSI can be taxed. If you are single or file separately, your 50- percent limit is $25,000 and your 85-percent limit is $34,000.

You might assume that it will be impossible to have a rich retirement and keep your income below those thresholds, but there are many types of income that aren't included in your MAGI.

Here's a partial list:

- Roth IRA income

- Return of principal from an annuity, life insurance or stock investment

- Cash borrowed from a whole life insurance policy

- Certain disability payments

- Health Savings Account contributions

- Student loan interest

- Educator expense

- Permitted self-employment taxes

- Permitted itemized deductions above the standard deduction including charitable deductions

- Death benefits from life insurance

- Cash advanced on a loan or mortgage

- Deferred income inside an annuity

Many sources of income are tax advantaged:

- Long-term capital gain treatment for appreciated stock or real estate when sold after one year and a day

- Real estate investments with depreciation

- Business or farm deductions

- Tax-qualified dividends taxed at 0% to 20%

- Municipal bond income

There are several other ways of reducing income from MAGI:

- Qualified deductible contributions to certain retirement plans.

- Certain oil and gas investments

- Tax credits as a rule don't affect MAGI

- Alimony payments are deductible to the paying spouse and taxable to the receiving spouse

- Defer income from retirement plans

If the total of one-half of your Social Security benefit and your MAGI exceeds your dollar amount limit (based on your income tax filing status), part of your Social Security benefit will be taxable.

Tax-free bond income is considered an addition to your AGI and MAGI when calculating whether your Social Security benefit is taxable. Be aware that this stealth tax can undo all the other good planning you might have done to receive tax-free income from Social Security.

Don't let this deter you from investing in tax-free bonds. The bottom line is still positive for higher-income retirees whose SSI is taxable anyway.

Always work with a qualified tax professional when making these calculations. Tax rules are complicated, easily misunderstood, changing constantly and don't necessarily make sense.

You are most likely going to reduce your MAGI by taking income from a Roth IRA or using principal from a prior investment. The most-taxed items on your return are income from individually owned certificates of deposit, employment income, interest income from a non-qualified annuity above cost basis, and withdrawals from a traditional IRA or other pre-tax retirement plan.

If you received an income deduction, deferral of taxes or depreciation tax benefit for putting the money into the plan or investment, the money will likely be taxable when you take it out. If you invested after-tax money, it's more likely to come to you tax free or tax advantaged.

It's possible for a single person or couple receiving SSI to reduce above-the-line income, especially those who own a business. Here are some potential deductions:

- Certain business expenses of reservists, performing artists, and fee-basis government officials

- Student loan interest

- Tuition and fees

- Investment losses up to $3,000 a year

- Educator expenses

- Self-employment expenses

- Rental property expenses

- Health savings accounts and Flexible Spending Accounts contributions

- One-half of self-employment tax

- Self-employed health insurance deduction

- Self-employed SEP, SIMPLE, and qualified-plan contributions

- Penalty on early withdrawal of savings

- Investment losses against gains; up to $3,000 each year against ordinary income

With a little planning you can control the taxes you pay during retirement so that you—not Washington—get to spend your hard-earned money. Set aside a few minutes now to begin small changes to your retirement savings plans so that, once you retire, you can retire as few others do. Lowering your taxes will allow you to get more bang for your retirement bucks than sending 22 percent or more to the IRS.

Conclusions

At this point, you should be convinced that your pauper brain has been defeated and you are now a wiser human being. You recognize the damage overspending inflicts on wealth building. Having too much stuff is a burden that will hold you back and keep you from reaching your goals.

By spending less, you conquer the debt problems that plague paupers. Living within your income and saving becomes easier every year.

Your personal life will undoubtedly run smoother. Relationships will be richer and more rewarding if everyone is on the same page. It's even easier to see occasional unemployment as a temporary reorganization rather than a halt to your way of life.

You should have the right amount of insurance for illness, disability or premature death so that your family won't be destitute should the unexpected occur. Working with a qualified fiduciary profession can made the process so much easier.

You should now be planning to have sufficient assets for a fulfilling retirement that starts when you want it to start. You should be saving enough now and making those small changes as early as possible to retire with manageable taxes.

Look around. You are now probably doing better than 90 percent of your peers. There's reason to celebrate. In appreciation, now is a good time to become an evangelist for proper financial planning. See if you can help others do the same. There are paupers everywhere that can use a kind word of advice.

Chapter Seven

Behavioral Finance

Investment professionals have been baffled by the irrational behavior of the financial markets since the beginning of time. We've discussed one of the first examples, the Tulip Mania of the 16th Century. It seems many times that there's more irrational stock market behavior than rational behavior.

The economists of the world would have you believe that the efficient market hypothesis (EMH) rules. EMH says that at any given time in a highly liquid market, stock prices are exactly matched to their value. This theory assumes that all participants in the stock market are attempting to try to maximize gains and reduce losses.

Another idea says that all stock market participants have complete knowledge of all information. All participants are rational, intelligent and acting to maximize success. All participants have access to the same information whether complete or flawed. The current price or "fair price" is the best price arrived by a liquid market at that given time.

The most brilliant minds in economics and finance have been unable to explain anomalies like bubbles and deep recessions. Most stock market participants can't explain the volatility that often plagues and baffles investors day by day or sometimes hourly.

I believe it's because humans are using the ancestral or pauper side of their brains and trading stocks like hunter gathers. The rules of buy low and sell high have seldom been followed during any volatile selloff.

John Maynard Keynes (1883-1946) founded most of our fundamental ideas about economics. His ideas about macroeconomics, governmental economic policies and business cycles make him the most influential economist of the 20th century.

The markets are moved by animal spirits, and not by reason.
John Maynard Keynes

During the Great Depression, he published his magnum opus, The General Theory of Employment, Interest, and Money. Even he couldn't explain why irrational behavior would occur, sometimes more often than rational behavior.

Recent research has focused on the illogical behavior exhibited in the stock markets and named this specialty Behavioral Finance or BF. BF is in direct contradiction to Efficient Market Hypothesis and Modern Portfolio Theory. This conflict is explained by studying a series of biases and psychological observations.

Statistical Analysis now allows us to accurately test the decisions of investors, analysts, investment advisors and academics to see how rational they turn out to be. The conclusions have been very unkind to all those who participated in those studies.

Psychological biases can help explain much of this irrational behavior. Physical and mental health can influence how an investor will feel about investing. We've been discussing that many illogical or irrational investment decisions are made by the gut feeling. Research seems to back this up.

A blindfolded monkey throwing darts at a newspaper's financial pages could select a portfolio that would do just as well as one carefully selected by experts.

Burton Malkiel

Here's a short list of the BF concepts that have been filling the headlines and selling many books lately:

Mental Accounting

Most people allocate their funds for specific purposes. People code, calculate, categorize and evaluate economic outcomes with Mental Accounting. Credit cards take advantage of the buyer by short circuiting mental accounting. If I pay cash, I don't buy it. If I charge it, I feel I didn't really spend that money, called transaction decoupling.

Mental Accounting short circuiting also allows American public policy to spend more. We now have a United States national debt above $31 trillion. If it were perceived this was real money, no policy maker or voter would allow this to take place.

Herd Behavior

Investors tend to mimic each other. Every rally or sell-off starts with herd behavior. Science finds an integrated approach to herding, describing two key issues: the mechanisms of transmission of the thoughts or behavior of individuals and connected patterns of behavior. Herding occurs in almost all forms of human behavior.

Emotional Gap

Many economic decisions are made under the strains of extreme emotions such as anxiety, anger, fear or excitement. There are ways to close the Emotional Gap that would contribute to better investment decisions, employment choices and personal relationships.

Anchoring

Many irrational spending behaviors are based on satisfaction as opposed to budgeting. Why else would anyone buy a $7 latte? Another aspect of Anchoring says that the first piece of information a person gets overwhelms everything that follows.

Anchoring has been shown to be an effective technique to persuade juries or judges to acquit or convict. Salesmen also use it. Anchoring can infiltrate something as simple as investing with a church, mosque or synagogue member. While investing with a church member isn't positive or negative, most of the money invested with Bernie Madoff came from members of his own faith.

Spotlight Effect

Investors that perceive a salesperson is talking directly at or to them are more apt to buy what is being sold. Test subjects tended to regard their importance to others significantly higher than the other participant. People believe they are being noticed more than they are. One is the center of their own world. The spotlight effect is the innate tendency to forget that although you indeed are the center of your world, you are not the center of anyone else's world.

Planning Fallacy

Humans tend to underestimate how much time should be devoted to planning and implementing a strategy and overestimate their ability to accomplish that task. The expanded definition of Planning Fallacy includes the tendency to underestimate the time, costs, and risks of future actions and to overestimate the benefits of the same actions.

This phenomenon can result in not only time overruns, but also cost overruns and benefit shortfalls. Investors underestimate the time it takes to allow an invested portfolio to grow, accumulate dividends and mature.

Instant results are often what is desired. This can result in gambling behaviors or selling winner stock picks too soon.

Self-Attribution
Most investors made decisions based on overconfidence of one's own knowledge and skills. Investors tend to rank their abilities above others, even when they fall short. Test subjects made systematic errors when evaluating or try to find reasons for their own and other's behaviors. Subjects made attributions or assumptions about why people behave in certain ways.

Rather than operating as objective perceivers, subjects tended to give a biased interpretation that fit their view of their social world. This can be observed in traffic situations.

A car changes lanes dangerously close to a person's car. The offended driver perceives the car is driven by a reckless, rude individual who purposefully cut them off. The driver of the car just didn't see them and had no evil intent.

Biases Revealed by Behavioral Finance

There are likely many biases that haven't been described or studied yet. BF has analyzed and studied several repeat biases. Here's a short list.

Confirmation Bias

Investors tend to seek out information that confirms their already accepted opinion. If information exists that confirms their choice, it is accepted readily. Contrary information is rejected as flawed.

This effect is stronger for emotionally charged issue and entrenched beliefs like politics or religion. CB can't be eliminated but can be managed by education and training in critical thinking skills.

Attitude polarization, belief perseverance, irrational primacy (reliance on information heard early in an argument), and illusory correlation or falsely perceived associations are some of the thought errors revealed during research on CB.

Optimism Bias or Pessimism Bias

Humans tend to have an exaggerated sense of optimism or pessimism depending on genes governing psychological traits and predispositions. Risk taking is a gene-governed trait, as is hair color and skin color. Environment and family can exaggerate this bias and investments can be affected.

OB is common in every gender, ethnicity, nationality, and age. OB are even reported in nonhuman animals such as rats and birds. The factors that govern OB include the subjects desired end state, their cognitive mechanisms, the information they have about themselves, others and the world and overall mood.

Pessimism Bias seems a little easier to explain. PB says that a negative result will happen regardless of the evidence presented. PB can affect investing by keeping a person in investments that have guarantees and lower returns.

Experiential Bias

Recent experiences seem more likely to happen again. 2008-2009 is an example of an economic event that caused many investors to permanently abandon stock investing. The Great Depression caused a whole generation of investors to shun stock investing.

EB assumes that because you've seen and experienced so much, that you know what's going to happen next. It's been called a killer by psychologists. In investing, no one can predict stock market moves in the future. After a protracted 50% stock market correction we should assume that the risk is lower. EB tells the brain that you could lose another 50%.

Loss Aversion

Many investors place a greater value in avoiding losses than contemplating stock market gains. It is irrational for investors to think they can reach their goals by selling winners and keeping losers, known as the disposition effect.

Investors are often reluctant to admit a mistake; instead, they will hang on to losers. These decisions usually harm their investment results. Subjects often would reply that they would keep a losing stock until it became a winner in contradiction to logic and their goals.

Familiarity Bias

Familiarity Bias is the tendency for individuals to be more comfortable with the familiar, dislike ambiguity, and dislike the unknown. The different types of FB can affect the individuals while others affect the advisor. Portfolio diversification and risk reduction usually suffer.

Many retirement portfolios over invest in the company or the industries where the future retirees work. CFP® professional guidelines suggest that no one company account for over 10% of a balanced portfolio and no industry should be over 20%. Some investors have a bias against oil, China, tobacco, liberal or conservative companies. These decisions often add risk and reduce investment results.

Conclusion from Behavioral Finance

Behavioral Finance principles are on display every day. Credit cards appeal to consumers to buy more to get 2% cash back. Grocery stores use gimmicks like oversized carts and continual layout changes and to get shoppers to load up their carts. Higher priced and full markup grocery items tend to be at eye level while the best priced and on sale items with less markup are on the top or bottom shelves. It's not a coincidence that highest markup impulse items are displayed near the check out.

BF is used ever time a consumer sees an item on sale. The retail on a shirt is $100. It's on sale for $49.99. Will we save $50.00 if we buy the shirt? People choose the AAA listing in the phone book over all other listings. There was a reason why Apple, Inc. chose AAPL as its stock symbol. People trust the algorithms of Google, an example of herd behavior.

The Buy one, Get One Free offer gets me every time. The real question I have for you? Why as an investor would you shun stock market investments when they are 50% off market highs? Logic would say that risk is lower than before the correction. BF says that the decision-making equipment, the investor's brain, tends to keep an investor from making a logical conclusion. The Homo pauperis brain wins again.

BF is used by every con artist and legitimate salesman. Every minister, politician, business leader and teacher use BF concepts to help convince members of their audience to exhibit herd mentality. As humans, we are hard wired to accept these messages, sometimes to our collective gain and sometimes to our individual loss as investors. BF is not good or bad but depends on the benevolent or evil intentions of the user.

There are several noteworthy conclusions here. The idea that the stock market is a logical place with rational actors making rational decisions can be thrown out the window. People tend to sell their winners way too soon and hold on to their losers way too long. Investors shun stocks on sale during a correction and load up on them during a stock market bubble.

The slow, steady, almost boring method of investing is almost always more successful than the fly-by-the-seat-of-your-pants approach most investors use. Emotion and gut feelings often rule the day when reasoned financial planning rarely gets a chance.

Some investors and advisors are successfully using Market Psychology technical indicators that help them judge the level of irrational behavior in the stock and bond markets at any given time. Seek out the logical fiduciary that will help you make logical and balanced market decisions consistent with your Investment Policy Statement.

The psychology that drives the market is indeed hard to predict. Come back to the mind of our ancient ancestors that still governs the reasoning of most investors. Fear, greed and "must have" desires govern more decisions than the reasoned, knowledgeable decision making of an intelligent investor.

I conclude that an investor's overall health governs more decisions than any other factor. Your stomach just feels off, you have a cold, you're mad at the traffic. These feelings shouldn't have anything to do with your investment decisions, provided you have a well-though out, balanced portfolio.

A solid financial plan with set well-defined goals can overcome any bias. You are the result of 100,000s if not 1,000,000s of years of evolution. Every one of your ancestors was a clever, successful adventurous fellow human that prevailed where others failed.

We prevail by learning. You've taken a huge step by reading this book. Set a goal to read a good financial book once a month or at least regularly. Great BF knowledge is available at every level of investment experience. You can benefit as a novice investor or the most experienced options trader.

Now get ready to get off your butt and start to plan to think and invest like the wise investor you are. You are a proud member of

Homo sapiens. Start investing like it. Get your investment policy statement updated to eliminate the BF mistakes you might have made in the past.

Every bias can be overcome or even used to make money from those that succumb to its herd behavior allure. Get ready to watch the financial news like you never have before. The Homo pauperis want you to buy their quality stocks cheap. Consider selling your losers quickly, hold your winners longer. The buy low, sell high strategy only works if you stop your own BF herd behavior.

Interpret bad news as "We are closer to the bottom" and my risk is lower. Interpret good news as "We are closer to the top and my risk is higher". A properly diversified portfolio will likely have less volatility in down markets than an over concentrated portfolio.

Chapter Eight

The Battle Plan

In this chapter, I hope to convey two important messages. First, I want you to sense the abundant opportunities that exist to take advantage of what Carl Icahn refers to as the "natural stupidity" of other investors. I also want to give you a battle plan to help you recognize that these opportunities exist in order to build personal wealth and security for you and your family.

Paupers are Vulnerable

Most other investors, other advisors, and Wall Street will give you ample opportunities to plunder their assets and doing so is perfectly legal. Time and again they will open their doors and their brokerage account for you. In fact, they will beg you to buy their good investments at rock-bottom prices.

They'll even buy your overpriced stocks at inflated prices. It's like going down to the Mercedes dealer and getting a new S Class for half price, then having the dealer offer to buy your trade-in for double its value. How long do you have to ponder about that exchange?

It may sound insane, but paupers want you to take advantage of their weaknesses. They will even tell you when it's time to come for the goodies, if you listen. The nightly news will shout it out; headlines in the paper will scream: "Record Low Dow Today." You will hear that volatility is rampant.

You will know all this is good, but paupers will think it's bad. And they will come running, hat in hand, beseeching you to buy their assets at steep discounts. It's the sale of the century.

Following is a list of opportunities sure to present themselves.

All you must do is be prepared with the correct response.

Opportunity: Many other investors and their advisors are most fearful and hesitant to invest when stock prices are lowest.

Your Response: Increase contributions to your 401k, or fund your IRA early that year. Consider moving some cash or conservative investments to an invested position or more aggressive investment. Think of this like horseshoes and hand grenades: just getting close to the bottom is usually good enough.

Opportunity: Paupers and their advisors are more likely to sell stock-based investments when stock prices are lowest.

Your Response: Determine if you own quality investments. If you do, resolve that you won't sell while the paupers are losing their heads. Assuming this is a low spot in a downturn, if you are comfortable and able to assume more risk, consider moving to more aggressive positions. For example, sell value stocks and buy growth stocks or emerging markets.

Opportunity: Stock prices are soaring. Paupers and their advisors are wildly optimistic and therefore more apt to buy stocks than sell.

Your Response: Examine your investments regularly to see which are selling at a profit. Put in a trailing stop loss[46] on stock more aggressive investments. You will get the upside should they continue to go up in price and be protected from a possible selloff. Sell half your position or enough to recoup your original investment and invest into a quality sector that has recently gone down in price.

Consider investing excess cash into high dividend value stocks. Rebalance your portfolio. This sells the overpriced assets and buys the underpriced assets. What we want to do is sell high and buy low,

Opportunity: Paupers, advisors and analysts predict that current trends will continue.

Your Response: No trend continues forever. Determine whether the trend is long or short range. Typical long-range trends are CD interest rates, mortgage rates and real estate prices. Short-range trends include stock market volatility or stock prices. At some point, every trend changes. Be protected by having the appropriate amount in negatively correlated assets.[47] A balanced portfolio of good quality investments will contain something that will rise as something else goes down, and you won't be hurt.

Opportunity: When faced with uncertainty, paupers will mimic the investment strategy of a friend, associate or family member— typically someone they respect as having more knowledge than they do. This is classic herd mentality.

Your Response: Sometimes the respected person is a smart investor, sometimes a pauper. Ask a few questions based on what you have learned in this book to find out. If a pauper, don't argue or try to change their thinking. It's hard to change their mind. If you have a pauper in your midst, simply do exactly the opposite of what they are doing.

Opportunity: Paupers would rather buy the stock of a familiar or "big name" company than a better-value company whose name they don't recognize.

Your Response: It's generally unwise to sink all your assets into one company, even if you work there. CERTIFIED FINANCIAL PLANNER™ Practitioners typically recommend a balanced portfolio of investments that include no more than 10 to 20 percent of your company's stock.

Opportunity: Paupers prefer to invest in stocks or funds that have experienced exceptional gains recently.

Your Response: Interpret a rising stock price as adding risk. Conversely, stocks or funds going down in price tend to reduce risk. Your balanced portfolio should contain positions that have experienced both. Rebalance your investments on a regular basis or when the portfolio has gained or lost 10 percent. Simply pick your trigger.

One approach is to reduce or sell your winners and move to low volatility or low-risk investments until a market correction occurs. You might also want to take a profit.

Opportunity: Paupers would rather "invest" in a big house or expensive car than put money into stock-market-based investments.

Your Response: Houses and cars are consumer goods. If yours are more expensive than they should be, it's like eating that 72-ounce steak; it's not going to go well. Consumer goods are rarely good investments. That $50,000 car may smell great when it's new but it will be a $5,000 trade-in 10 to 15 years later. If your home is twice as large as you need, its upkeep and repairs or overhead will be double as well.

Opportunity: Paupers feel secure when they have an expensive wardrobe or home furnishings.

Your Response: Our society constantly cajoles you to consume. Paupers over consume. They consume first and save if anything is leftover. Resolve to save at least the first 10 percent of your income. Start with an emergency fund savings account, work up to saving in your retirement plan, and eventually add 529 education plans for your children.

Add on the appropriate amount of life and long term care insurance when affordable, and adjust as needed. Try not to go into debt except for your primary residence. Try to spend no more than 28 percent of your income for mortgage or rent. Less would be better.

Opportunity: Paupers spend more time planning vacations or landscaping their yards than they do on investment and retirement planning.

Your Response: I like yard work and vacations too, but unlike paupers, I don't avoid discussions about investing. I recommend you vow to read at least one or two quality investment books every year. A list of my recommendations to sharpen your financial saw appears at the end of this book. I also recommend that you have regular family budget meetings.

Opportunity: Some of the smartest and best-educated investors make the same mistakes that average investors make.

Your Response: Paupers come in all ages, and some are brilliant people, but they are paupers and vulnerable to being exploited. The pauper buffet of opportunity will probably never end because they repeat the same mistakes. Find the right rhythm and you can profit, as have many of the world's wealthiest investors.

Opportunity: The average investment advisor often makes the same mistakes as the average investor.

Your Response: Many advisors are also paupers. Beware of advisors who prey upon the fear or greed of paupers. Find an advisor with at least five years of experience and a CFP® professional designation.

If you engage an advisor who acts as your fiduciary,[48] you are more likely to get an unbiased presentation that will disclose all material facts and produce a plan that is in your best interest.

Without these standards, you may be investing with an untrained advisor who might place the interests of his company over yours. Worse, there are crooks that out-and-out lie and steal.

Opportunity: When presented with conflicting information, paupers shut down, afraid to do anything.

Your Response: The world is full of conflicting information. If you have the right advisor, he or she will watch out for you. It's best if you have a policy statement for both hiring and firing an advisor and investing. These policy statements are best produced when emotions are low and bring clarity to decisions when chaos abounds.

Opportunity: Paupers who experience a significant loss will avoid similar stocks, going forward.

Your Response: All cycles and selloffs repeat themselves. They always have. According to the National Bureau of Economic Research, the U.S. has encountered 32 cycles of expansions and contractions over the past 150 years, with an average of 17 months of contraction and 38 months of expansion.

Occurring on average every five years, recessions are typically accompanied by a 20 percent or more sell off in global investment markets. Between recessions, four to eight selloffs of 10 percent or more occur. During the 20 years of January 1994, through January, 2014, the Dow rose from 3978 to 15,699, despite some serious problems and several historically significant recessions. Selloffs remain as common as dirt. Paupers see them as problems; you should think of them as opportunities.

Opportunity: You are probably not as good an investor as you think you are.

Your Response: Behavioral Finance shows that we are riddled with biases. We tend to recall making better decisions than we did. Paupers have a tough time recalling their investing errors. It's only natural. Our ancestors tried to forget how close they came to extinction. Set up a discipline to track your investment results and review it quarterly.

Create a Strong Foundation

A process that helps you resist the temptation to sell low and buy high will protect you from backsliding. A competent professional planner can help you implement your process. The two most respected designations are CFP® professional CERTIFIED FINANCIAL PLANNER™ Practitioner and AIF® (Accredited Investment Fiduciary).

To avoid being "sold" investments, establish a relationship with a trusted advisor who will assume fiduciary responsibility and do the following:

- Define your professional relationship

- Gather all your data and discuss your goals

- Analyze and evaluate your current financial status

- Present appropriate recommendations and alternatives

- Implement the recommendations

- Monitor the recommendations

- Educate and explain what's happening and why the investment markets are doing what they are doing.

Your advisor's fiduciary responsibility is a vital part of your agreement or contract. You should have a frank discussion about how your advisor will be compensated and how fees will be paid. What specifically will your advisor be doing on your behalf? Will your advisor have discretion to trade your account?

If you choose to be your own advisor, you must be willing to accept that same level of responsibility. Here's what you will need to know and do before you decide to go it alone:

- Knowledge of the tax system as administered by the IRS and your state of residence

- Knowledge of the investments that might be used in your plan

- Knowledge of estate plans, wills, trusts and powers of attorney

- Knowledge of life insurance, annuities and long-term care policies.

- Evaluate and understand the current condition of your finances

- Develop a cash flow statement: know when you will need money and when you will receive money

- Understand your debt: how much you owe and to whom, what it's costing you and when it must be paid back.

Try not to be overwhelmed. This is going to be a lifelong task. Tackle one step at a time. See the appendix of this book for a suggested reading list.

Congratulations

Having made it this far, you now view finances and investing in a whole new light. You can be assured you are no longer a pauper. You can now take full advantage of your new status as a Homo sapiens. You are ready to profit from your new knowledge. Be patient, my friend. The opportunities will present themselves soon enough.

Suggested Reading List

One of my goals each year is to read and understand several good books on financial planning, tax planning, behavioral investing, and economics. Most of the research for my book came from prior significant reading in this treasure trove of knowledge. If you have time to dive into another book or two, you could choose from my suggested reading list.

Animal Spirits: How Human Psychology Drives the Economy, George A. Akerlof, Robert J. Shiller

Behavioral Economics Third Ed., Edward Cartwright

Behavioral Investment Counseling, Nick Murray

Beyond the Random Walk, Vijay Singal

Contrarian Investment Strategies: The Psychological Edge, David Dreman

How to Write an Investment Policy Statement, Jack Gardner and Donald B. Trone

Irrational Exuberance, Robert J. Shiller

Rich Dad Poor Dad, Robert T. Kiyosaki

Smart Couples Finish Rich, David Bach

Smart Women Finish Rich, David Bach

Super Cycles, Arun Motianey

The Little Book of Behavioral Investing, James Montier

The Richest Man in Babylon, George Clason

The Savage Number, How Much Money Do You Need to Retire, Terry Savage

The Wealthy Barber, David Chilton

Understanding Exchange Traded Funds, Archie M. Richards, Jr.

Why It Matters for Global Capitalism, George A. Akerlof, Robert J. Shiller

Your Money and Your Brain, Jason Zweig

Endnotes

Introduction

1 Will Lassek, Steve Gaulin, and Hara Estroff Marano, "Eternal Curves," Psychology Today, 3 July 2012.

Ch1

2 Positron emission tomography (PET) is a nuclear medicine imaging which produces a three-dimensional image or picture of functional processes in the body and brain.

3 A valuation ratio of a company's current share price compared to its per-share earnings.

4 Endorphins are opioid compounds produced by the pituitary gland and hypothalamus. They have an effect on the brain much like opium or morphine. These chemicals are released during moments of excitement, pain and strenuous exercise. They are responsible for the feelings of euphoria during a "runner's high" and even orgasm.

5 Unsustainable investor enthusiasm that drives asset prices up to levels that aren't supported by fundamentals. The term "irrational exuberance" is believed to have been coined by Alan Greenspan in a 1996 speech, "The Challenge of Central Banking in a Democratic Society." He said that low inflation reduces investor uncertainty, lowers risk premiums and implies higher stock market returns. Also see Robert J. Shiller's classic behavioral investing book, Irrational Exuberance.

Ch2

6 Robert M. Sapolsky, Why Zebras Don't Get Ulcers (1994, Holt/Owl 3rd Rep. Ed. 2004)

7 The fight-or-flight response, also known as the acute stress response, refers to a physiological reaction that occurs in the presence of something that is terrifying, either mentally or physically. The fight-or- flight response was first described in the 1920s by American physiologist Walter Cannon. Cannon realized that a chain of rapidly occurring reactions inside the body help mobilize the body's resources to deal with threatening

circumstances. Source: Kendra Cherry, "What is the Fight-or-Flight Response?" www.psychology.about.com.

8 Superimposed upon seasonal changes in morphology, physiology and behavior, are facultative responses to unpredictable events known as labile (i.e., short-lived) perturbation factors (LPFs). These responses include behavioral and physiological changes that enhance survival and collectively make up the "emergency" life history stage. Source: John Wingfield, Donna Maney, Creagh Breuner, Jerry Jacobs, Sharon Lynn, Marilyn Ramenofsky and Ralph Richardson, "Ecological Bases of Hormone—Behavior Interactions: The Emergency Life History Stage," Integrative & Comparative Biology, Vol 38, Issue 1, pp 191-206.

Ch 3

9 Also known as the Dow 30, the DJIA is an index that shows how 30 large publicly owned companies based in the United States have traded during a standard trading session in the stock market.

10 Paul Kosakowski, "Financial Markets: Random, Cyclical Or Both?" 8 Dec 2013.

11 The yield curve is a graph that plots time (from shortest to longest maturity date) on the horizontal access, and yield on the vertical access. It is used to show the relationship between yield and maturity. Source: www.learnbonds.com.

12 A Put is an option contract giving the owner the right, but not the obligation, to sell a specified amount of an underlying asset at a set price within a specified time. The buyer of a put option estimates that the underlying asset will drop below the exercise price before the expiration date.

13 Roughly speaking, quantitative easing refers to changes in the composition and/or size of a central bank's balance sheet that are designed to ease liquidity and/or credit conditions. Source: Alan S. Blinder, "Quantitative Easing: Entrance and Exit Strategies" Federal Reserve Bank of St. Louis, Nov/Dec 2010: p465.

14 Annual Returns on Stock, T. Bonds and T. Bills: 1928 – Current, New York University Stern, 5 Jan 2014.

15 Anna Prior, "The Hidden Costs of Mutual Funds," The Wall Street Journal, 1 March 2010.

16 Nick Murray, Behavioral Investment Counseling, 2008: p29.

Ch4

17 Dorothy Cheney and Robert Seyfarth, How Monkeys See The World: Inside The Mind of Another Species, University of Chicago Press, 1992.

18 CBOE data for the VIX volatility index supply March 1, 2004, to March 1, 2014.

19 A flash crash is a very rapid, deep, and volatile fall in security prices occurring within an extremely short time period. A flash crash frequently stems from trades executed by black-box trading, combined with high-frequency trading, whose speed and interconnectedness nature can result in the loss and recovery of billions of dollars in a matter of minutes and seconds.

20 G. A. Akerlof and R. J. Shiller, Animal Spirits: How Human Psychology Drives the Economy, and Why It Matters for Global Capitalism, Princeton University Press.

21 "The article notes that gold prices, just over $1600 an ounce yesterday, are now about 17% below their all-time high (in nominal terms) of $1920 an ounce set almost a year ago last September." Source: Financial Times London, 17 August, 2012.

Ch5

22 Sriram Sankararaman, "The Date of Interbreeding between Neanderthals and Modern Humans," Journal of Postnatal Genetics, 04 Oct. 2012.

23 Moore's law is the observation that, over the history of computing hardware, the number of transistors on integrated circuits doubles approximately every two years.

24 Alexander E.M. Hess, "Countries with the Most Millionaires," USA Today 17 Sept. 2013.

25 Julian D. Richards, Viking Age England (London: B.T. Batsford and English Heritage 1991: 9.

26 The term "emerging markets" refers to the markets of countries that are at an early stage of their development, relative to the mature markets of countries like the United States or Japan. Emerging markets are typically much smaller than their developed counterparts and such markets tend to be less well established than mainstream markets, often with less comprehensive regulations around how companies and investors can operate. (www.qfinance.com)

27 A developing country, also called a less-developed country (LDC) is a nation with a lower living standard, underdeveloped industrial base, and low Human Development Index (HDI) relative to other countries. There is no universal, agreed-upon criterion for what makes a country developing versus developed and which countries fit these two categories. (www.qfinance.com)

Ch 6

28 F Cavazzi, "The Roman Army," Roman-Empire.net, 8 April 2012.

29 Dora L Costa, The Evolution of Retirement: An American Economic History, 1880-1990 (University of Chicago Press, January 1998).

30 Walter Updegrave, "Do I Really Need My Savings to Last Until I'm 100?" Money 27 April 2012.

31 Jennie Phipps, "Living on Social Security Alone," Bankrate.com 17 Sept. 2012.

32 If you withdraw money from a Roth IRA and you are under age 59½, you will not be taxed or pay a penalty on the contributions you withdraw, but your earnings will be taxed as income and you will pay a penalty tax on the income, unless you own the account for at least five years and you meet one of the exceptions.

33 Refers to stocks with a relatively small market capitalization. The definition of small cap can vary among brokerages, but generally it is a company with a market capitalization of between $300 million and $2 billion.

34 Refers to companies with market capitalization between $2 and $10 billion, which is calculated by multiplying the number of a company's shares outstanding by its stock price. Mid cap is an abbreviation for the term "middle capitalization."

35 A term used by the investment community to refer to companies with a market capitalization value of more than $10 billion. Large cap is an abbreviation of the term "large market capitalization." Market capitalization is calculated by multiplying the number of a company's shares outstanding by its stock price per share.

36 A nation's economy that is progressing toward becoming advanced, as shown by some liquidity in local debt and equity markets and the existence of some form of market exchange and regulatory body. Emerging markets generally do not have the level of market efficiency and strict standards in accounting and securities regulation on par with advanced economies (such as the United States, Europe and Japan), but emerging markets will

typically have a physical financial infrastructure including banks, a stock exchange and a unified currency.

37 A measure of the sensitivity of the price (the value of principal) of a fixed-income investment to a change in interest rates. Duration is expressed as a number of years. Rising interest rates mean falling bond prices, while declining interest rates mean rising bond prices.

38 Philip L Cooley, Carl M Hubbard and Daniel T Walz, "Sustainable Withdrawal Rates From Your Retirement Portfolio" Association for Financial Counseling and Planning Education.

39 Ibid. This study reports the effects of a range of nominal and inflation- adjusted withdrawal rates applied monthly on the success rates of retirement portfolios of large-cap stocks and corporate bonds for payout periods of 15, 20, 25 and 30 years. A portfolio is deemed a success if it completes the payout period with a terminal value that is greater than zero. Using historical financial market returns, the study suggests that portfolios of at least 75% stock provide 4% to 5% inflation-adjusted withdrawals.

40 Sheyna Steiner, "Americans plan to work through retirement," bankrate.com.

41 According to the IRS, taxable earned income includes:
- Wages, salaries, tips, and other taxable employee pay;
- Union strike benefits;
- Long-term disability benefits received prior to minimum retirement age;
- Net earnings from self-employment if:
- You own or operate a business or a farm or
- You are a minister or member of a religious order
- You are a statutory employee and have income.

42 The activities of daily living are basic, routine tasks, such as bathing, dressing, eating, taking medications, doing tranfers (getting from one chair to another) and using the toilet; activities that most people are able to perform on a daily basis without assistance.

43 USLegal.com.

44 Legal Information Institute, Cornell University Law School.

45 MAGI stands for Modified Adjusted Gross Income. Your MAGI is determined by subtracting from (or not including in) your adjusted gross income (AGI) the taxable amount of your Social Security benefit, and adding back in any income that is normally excludable

from your AGI, such as foreign earned income, and income from qualified U.S. savings bonds.

Ch 8

46 A complex stop-loss in which the stop loss price is set at some fixed percentage below the market price. If the market price rises, the stop loss price rises proportionately, but if the stock price falls, the stop loss price doesn't change. This technique allows an investor set a limit on the maximum possible loss without setting a limit on the maximum possible gain, and without requiring paying attention to the investment on an ongoing basis.

47 Correlation describes the movement relationship between two different assets. Two assets that move in the same direction are deemed to be positively correlated. On the other hand, if the two assets move in opposite directions, they are negatively correlated.

48 The term fiduciary refers to a relationship in which one person has a responsibility of care for the assets or rights of another person. A fiduciary is an individual who has this responsibility. A fiduciary relationship exists with individuals who handle money or property for others.

CPSIA information can be obtained
at www.ICGtesting.com
Printed in the USA
JSHW061751061222
34385JS00001B/2